Candlemaking for Profit

T0266672

Praise for this book...

This book is a rare thing in its ability to combine the practical and the creative. It is a practical guide that takes the reader through all they need to know to run a profitable and sustainable business. Yet it also avoids too many prescriptive directions and inspires the potential entrepreneur to be truly creative with their ideas. It gets the balance just right between telling you what you need to know, and what you need to discover for yourself through your own artistic and entrepreneurial endeavour. I am sure it will inspire businesses of many different types – from those mainly concerned with production of candles as practical household items to those looking to produce high-value design-led products.

John Miller, Director of MARK Product Ltd

'This practical guide to candlemaking will be welcomed by craftsmen and technical instructors alike. Not only does this valuable book cover the important technical aspects of candle making, it includes business considerations such as feasibility studies and business planning – essential undertakings in establishing a sustainable and competitive business. Building from first-hand experience in the craft as well as extensive knowledge of small enterprise in developing economies, Robert Aley has produced a text that is hugely practical and eminently readable.'

Kieron Crawley, Small enterprise consultant, with 20 years' experience in East Africa, Southern Africa, the Caribbean and Asia

'My own experience of supporting and running small enterprises in Africa highlights the importance of rigorous business planning and effective marketing to ensure success. I'm therefore delighted that Rob Aley has emphasized profit and viability from the title onwards in this clearly written guide, as well as communicating his enthusiasm for design and production. It's my sincere hope that readers of this book will not only create well-made and perhaps beautiful candles, but also incomes and employment where they are most needed.'

Andrew Betts, Director, Advantage Africa

Candlemaking for Profit

A practical guide for small-scale producers

Robert Aley

PRACTICAL ACTION
Publishing

Practical Action Publishing Ltd
The Schumacher Centre
Bourton on Dunsmore, Rugby,
Warwickshire CV23 9QZ, UK
www.practicalactionpublishing.org

ISBN 978 1 85339 721 9

Since 1974, Practical Action Publishing has published and disseminated
books and information in support of international development work
throughout the world. Practical Action Publishing is a trading name
of Practical Action Publishing Ltd (Company Reg. No. 1159018), the
wholly owned publishing company of Practical Action. Practical Action
Publishing trades only in support of its parent charity objectives and any
profits are covenanted back to Practical Action (Charity Reg. No. 247257,
Group VAT Registration No. 880 9924 76).

Cover photo: Robert Aley
Typeset by S.J.I. Services, New Delhi
Printed by CLE Print Ltd on FSC Mixed Source Paper

Contents

Figures

Tables

Photos

About the author

Robert Aley has run his own successful candlemaking business since 2003. The Wax Studio is a multi-award winning small business which has built a strong reputation for its innovative candle designs and handmade product quality. Robert Aley has a master's degree in design and extensive experience in advising small enterprises in developing countries.

Mindy Chillery co-owns The Wax Studio and has particular expertise in business planning and the costing and marketing of candles.

CHAPTER 1

The history of candlemaking
with contributions from Mindy Chillery

The basic principles of how a candle works have changed very little over the centuries, however the materials used and the production methods employed, have evolved and developed appreciably over time. Candles were originally used simply as a means of generating essential light, but gradually they became increasingly significant elements of spirituality and ceremony across many cultures and religions of the world. At one time candles were even employed as a means of time keeping. Advances in the materials used to make candles have been the main factor behind improvements, not only in their luminosity and cleanliness, but also in affordability, and people's desire to use them as ornamental items. Nowadays candles are still commonly used for utilitarian purposes in parts of the world that lack electricity, but in richer countries they have become more of a decorative item used for atmospheric light at home, or on special occasions.

The earliest candles

In ancient Egypt a type of wickless candle (or torch) was being made to provide light at night as early as 3150 BC. The ancient Egyptians used to cut naturally occurring rushes, peel back the outer stem and soak the core of the plant in melted animal fat and possibly beeswax. When set hard this was burnt like a small torch to produce light. Historic evidence of the existence of similar basic wickless candles appears to show that they were being produced independently and simultaneously in several of the world's early civilisations. In about 200 BC the ancient Chinese were using whale fat in a similar way to the Egyptians and along with the Japanese they used natural high fat produce such as nuts, seeds and insects as fuel for torch-like candles wrapped in rice paper. In other parts of the world people were using different fuels which were locally available to them. Yak's milk butter was used in Tibet for hundreds of years, whilst in India, Hindu temples were adorned with candles made from fuel derived from boiled cinnamon. On the north-west coast of North America they made use of an extraordinary local fish. The 'candlefish' was so fatty it could be simply dried and burnt on a stick to produce a convenient light source.

The Romans and the Middle Ages

The Romans are generally credited with making the first candles with wicks. They probably used papyrus reeds as the first wicks and tallow (animal fat) as the fuel. Although tallow was a readily available and practical solid fuel source, it was also unpleasant to work with and emitted nasty odours and smoke when it was burnt, due to its glycerine content. Despite these drawbacks, tallow went on to become the standard candlemaking material throughout the Middle Ages. These kinds of candles also became important in ceremonies and special occasions, such as Candlemas (the presentation of Jesus to God in the Temple at Jerusalem) and during Saint Lucy festivities (St Lucy's overcoming of darkness with light).

During the Anglo-Saxon period candlemaking had become sophisticated enough for candles to be used for time keeping. King Alfred the Great (849–899 AD) used a candle-clock that burned for a total of four hours and had simple lines around the side to show the passing of each hour. Later, 24-hour candles were invented based on the same concept. The Sung Dynasty in China (960–1279 AD) went on to develop elaborate time-keeping candles that included chiming mechanisms and even changed the aroma they produced at certain time intervals.

It was probably not until the Middle Ages that beeswax started to become more commonly used as a candlemaking material. This wax is naturally produced by honey bees and shaped into hexagonal honeycombs into which the bees deposit and store their honey. When the honey is harvested, the wax can be removed and cleaned for use in making candles. Beeswax candles were a marked improvement over those made with tallow, because they did not produce a smoky flame, or emit an acrid odour when burned. Instead, beeswax candles burned purely and cleanly, and also produced a pleasant honey scent. Beeswax, however, was far less readily available than tallow and this meant that it could be sold at a high price. Beeswax candles therefore became the preserve of rich individuals and institutions like the church where they were used for royal events. To this day, beeswax remains a highly valued premium candlemaking material.

More recent history

In Britain, the candlemaking profession became more formally recognized in the 1400s with the formation of the Worshipful Company of Wax Chandlers in about 1330. This was one of over 100 livery companies that originally developed as guilds. They were also responsible for the regulation of trade standards such as wage levels and labour conditions. The Wax Chandlers' Company was appointed a Royal Charter by Richard III in 1484, and is still in existence to this day. By the late 18th century a new candle-making wax became available in large volumes as a result of the expansion of the whaling industry. This was spermaceti, a wax made from the crystallization of sperm whale oil. Not only was this substance available in large quantities, but it made candles that were harder and thus kept their shape better in warm conditions. Another advantage of spermaceti was that, when burnt, it did not produce the repulsive smell of other animal fats such as tallow. However, like beeswax, candles produced from spermaceti were still expensive and further alternative materials were sought.

At this time candlemaking was also becoming increasingly indus-trialized. In 1790 the second US patent was granted to J.S. Sampson of Boston for a new method of candlemaking. Furthermore, even better alternative materials were discovered. Colza oil, derived from the plant *Brassica campestris*, and a similar oil, derived from rapeseed, were much cheaper alternatives to whale fat and made candles that produced bright smokeless flames.

The advent of paraffin wax

In the first half of the 19th century the hugely important discovery of paraffin wax was made, and it has remained the most common candle wax to this day. It was first produced in 1830, by French chemist Auguste Laurent by distilling bituminous shale. Just five years later another French chemist, Jean Dumas, devised a means of obtaining paraffin from coal-tar, but it was not until 1850 that paraffin wax become commercially viable, when James Young patented the process of producing it from coal. Then, in 1854, George Wilson of Prices Candles in London made the most important advance, when he produced paraffin wax from distilled petroleum oil. Paraffin wax had many advantages, it was clean, easy to handle, burnt well, and was relatively cheap. However, it did have one drawback. Used on its own it had a tendency to melt quickly and cause excessive dripping because of its low melting point. It was therefore a lucky coincidence that a few years earlier in 1811 a new and very hard slow-burning substance had been discovered and patented. This substance was stearic acid (also known as stearin), and when mixed with paraffin wax, made the perfect candlemaking material. By the end of the 19th century almost all candles were being produced from a blend of paraffin and stearin waxes.

The most important candlemaking company of the period was Prices, set up in 1830 by William Wilson and his partner Benjamin Lancaster. They called the company Edward Price and Co, deliberately avoiding the use of their own names. At that time in Britain it would have been disapproved of by the middle classes for a merchant to become involved in a lowly trade, especially one that was still associated with the butchery and foul odours of the tallow candle industry. Under his pseudonym 'Mr Price' took less than 20 years to become a household name and by 1900 the company was the largest maker of candles in the world. It made inexpensive stearin candles that burned almost as well as those made from costly beeswax. In 1834, Joseph Morgan had already begun to industrialize the production of candles. He invented a moulding machine, which manufactured 1,500 candles per hour. Prices introduced these mass production methods and this enabled the already successful company to go onto dominate the nightlight market.

Despite the advances in materials and mechanization throughout the 1800s, candle manufacturing was dealt its harshest blow in the later part of the century, when the oil industry started to develop superior new fuels, especially kerosene which was an excellent fuel for lamplights. Kerosene sales devastated the candle business. James Wilson of Prices was prompted to write in 1879, 'This flood of American petroleum poured in upon us by millions of gallons, giving light at a fifth of the cost of the cheapest candle.' The candle making industry was about to be changed forever. The introduction of oil-based fuel, the advent of the electric light bulb in 1879 and the wide-spread use of electricity, further reduced the demand for candles and kerosene in the industrialized nations of the world. Kerosene, the fuel that was responsible for the demise of the mass candlemaking industry, was in turn replaced by electricity and the convenience of light at the flick of a switch.

Modern times

To this day, electricity has by no means reached all parts of the world. In many developing countries candles remain important as a practical source of light. There are still 1.6 billion people lacking access to electricity. Most of these people live in rural locations and for them access to kerosene and candles as a functional light source remains important. Additionally, many of the world's poorer towns and cities still have unreliable power supplies and their inhabitants also need alternative temporary light sources. This market for utilitarian candles is now largely supplied by mass production taking place in India and China. For the rest of the world's inhabitants, those lucky enough to have reliable access to electricity, candles have become a non-essential luxury. The candle industry has moved towards producing decorative products designed to enhance people's feeling of wellbeing and relaxation. Developments in candlemaking materials continue to evolve, especially in the areas of natural and non-polluting waxes. In 1996 a 100 per cent soya wax was developed by extracting oil from soya beans and then hydrogenating it to make the first solid stable wax of this kind. Candlemakers have also started returning to some of the other natural waxes first used centuries ago, such as those made from rape-seed oil. Scented candles are also a relatively recent innovation in candle design, and now form a significant part of the luxury end of the market.

Candles have been in use by human civilizations since ancient times, and although they are no longer our main source of light they still hold significant cultural value. They remain very important components of traditional ceremony and spiritual ritual in churches, temples and most religious institutions worldwide. Whether it is the tradition of candles on a birthday cake, religious festivals like the eight candles of Hanukkah, or candles lit to commemorate people who have died at war, the symbolic flame of a burning candle is still an important component of many customs and practices.

CHAPTER 2

Feasibility study

with contributions from Mindy Chillery

This chapter explains why a feasibility study is essential, how to conduct a feasibility study for a small-scale candlemaking business and how to apply its findings to assist in making business decisions.

Why do a feasibility study?

A person with a new small enterprise idea will often be brimming with enthusiasm and optimism and be very keen to get the business up and running without delay. Whilst this eagerness and energy is very positive, you must also be careful not to dash into something that has not been properly considered and well researched. The tendency to rush into ill-conceived and costly business activities is one of the reasons why a high percentage of new businesses fail in the first few years. To minimise this risk of failure, it is essential to allocate time and effort to carefully research all the relevant aspects of the proposed business idea before the real work begins. This process of analysing and accessing a business idea before it is set up, is known as a feasibility study. The purpose of the feasibility study is not to 'confirm' that you have a great business idea, but to provide an objective analysis which will tell you and other people whether or not the business idea is viable, and if it is, the best ways to develop the new enterprise. Remember that the feasibility study might suggest that your idea is not as promising as you thought, in which case be prepared to pay attention to the results. You may need to abandon, adapt or further research your plans accordingly.

How to conduct a feasibility study

Typically a feasibility study is comprised of three sections:

- Stage 1: Market feasibility
- Stage 2: Technical feasibility
- Stage 3: Financial feasibility

Stage 1: Market feasibility

This is the first and critical stage of the feasibility study. The purpose is to establish if there is a genuine demand for the candles you are proposing to make and sell. If there is not, you will quite simply never have a viable business. This stage of the study will also inform you about the size and nature of the market into which you will be selling. Additionally, it should provide information on how to promote and sell your products, and information about your competitors, so as to determine your prospective market share.

Identify and research your customers

Firstly you need to determine whether you intend to sell your candles direct to the final user (end customer), or to a retailer or wholesaler who will sell them on to the end customer. Typically a small-scale candle enterprise will usually sell a proportion of their products direct to the end customer, perhaps through their own shop or website, and a proportion to the trade (retailers).

Whoever you think your customers will be, it is essential to research the requirements that they will place on your products and services in the future. To do this you have to establish what your customers are like. At first it may seem to you that almost everybody is a potential candle customer and therefore it is impossible to know where to start. It is therefore useful to begin by defining your *ideal* customer or client.

For example, if you are planning to produce candles that are particularly decorative, your customers will probably be people with an appreciation of design and an interest in interior decoration. They may be people who buy gifts or who appreciate luxury or handmade products, and they will probably be people with a relatively high disposable income. Gradually a customer profile will emerge. This will not encompass all your customers but will allow you to identify a group of individuals which you can use for more focused research. Now, you can identify individuals who fall within your ideal customer profile and conduct a simple market survey to find out more about what they like and dislike about your proposed products and services.

At this stage you will need some product samples and prices to show prospective customers so that their responses can be recorded. First ask them to give you their general impressions of what they see. Tell them to be absolutely honest in their responses (you are not looking for compliments!). Pay attention to and note down what they say. Then ask them a list of questions so that you get a more in depth understanding of their views. For example ask them:

- What candles they buy at the moment?
- How many they buy?
- How often and at what price?
- Is the size/shape/colour to their liking?
- Would they buy for themselves or as a gift? For what occasion?
- Is the packaging appropriate, what about box sets?
- What shops would they expect to stock them?
- Would they buy from a website?
- Is there anything they would change?

A similar consultation exercise can be undertaken with other customer groups, including any trade and wholesale customers. These potential customers are likely to take a more commercially orientated look at your business proposition. Although they will always be open to new and innovative products, they will also need to be convinced that you are able to provide a professional, reliable service. You should find out what they require in terms of stock availability, delivery times and payment terms. You can also ask them to estimate their likely order quantities. This in turn will give you an estimation of how many stockists you will require for sufficient income. It will also help with production planning.

The market study should be a short exercise so as to keep costs low. Keep it relevant and make good use of the information gathered from potential customers. Remember again to pay proper attention to suggestions and criticisms that your potential customers make and if the responses are negative, try to have the courage to adapt or even ditch your ideas. However if reactions are broadly positive you can begin to estimate the size and nature of the demand for your products. Some trade institutions (such as the Chambers of Commerce in the UK) conduct research into the size and value of whole market sectors. This information can assist enterprises to plan their marketing and production and is especially useful when larger businesses are estimating potential for sales expansion and increased market share. However for smaller enterprises, estimates of national and international market sector values are less relevant.

Identify and research your competitors

Your competitors are other businesses that are offering the same or similar products or services to your own. First of all, identify who are your real competitors. If you are planning to supply candles to a local market, then a business doing the same thing many miles away is, in reality, not really a competitor. Even a business in your local area offering similar products may not be a competitor if they are targeting a different customer group to you. Try to identify what your competitors do well and where they may have gaps or weaknesses that you can fill. Here are some useful things to learn about your main competitors:

- their name and location (or website);
- the type, quality and price of their products;
- their target customers;
- their marketing literature;
- how they promote themselves;
- any offers or incentives they offer to their customers;
- their size and structure;
- the similarities between your planned business and theirs.

Also consider:

- Why customers might change to buy your products instead of those of your competitors?
- What are your competitors likely to do if you introduce new products to the market?

Be wary of trying to compete head on with your competitors by offering an identical product but at a lower price. Many new businesses assume that if they can simply undercut their competitor they will seize the market share. This is a dangerous over simplification. Your competitors' loyal customers are unlikely to switch supply on price alone if the new business is unproven or the service is inferior. Also if you are inexperienced you may have slightly miscalculated your true business costs, and find it harder to compete on price than you originally anticipated. Remember, one of the best ways to compete with other businesses is to offer something new and different, especially if it is something your competitors will find difficult to copy and reproduce themselves.

Stage 2: Technical feasibility

Some new candlemaking entrepreneurs will already have knowledge and experience in the technical aspects of the business. Many will be intending to convert a hobby into a new enterprise. If you have no previous candlemaking experience you will need to identify training, or to work with an existing artisan to learn the essential skills required. For those who do have some technical experience, the areas of marketing, financial management and business administration may be less familiar than the candlemaking process itself. The scale of production for a viable business will also be a new challenge. Having established the size of the market available to your business, you will need to consider whether you are capable of producing the candles in the required quantities and at the correct quality and price in order to meet the demand. It may be that in the first year you will not intend to meet all of the potential demand for your products, but will plan to build your capacity to do this gradually over subsequent years. Consider:

- Location, size and cost of premises required.
- Design and making expertise.
- Equipment needed to meet the scale of production selected.
- Labour needed to meet the scale of production selected and training needs.
- Raw materials required, cost and availability of suppliers.

(See also Chapters five and six for further discussion on these aspects).

Stage 3: Financial feasibility

It is impossible to decide whether or not you have a viable business idea unless you have a clear overview of the initial start-up costs, operational costs and projected income. Your feasibility study will begin to allow you to make these essential financial estimates before any of your money is invested.

Initial set-up costs (capital costs)

Set-up costs are those associated with establishing the business before the conventional daily production, marketing and sales begin. Typically, these will include the purchase of workshop equipment (known as capital equipment), the purchase of a vehicle if required and the purchase of premises, if you are not renting. Fortunately small candlemaking enterprises can start off by keeping these costs relatively low as compared to other small manufacturing businesses. The cost of the necessary equipment and tools is fairly low, and in practice many people will start-up their businesses on their own premises or by renting a modest sized workshop, which they can vacate as the business expands.

On-going costs

You will have two types of on-going costs:

- Fixed costs (also known as overheads or indirect costs) – these are costs that you will incur just because your business exists, whether or not you actually make or sell any candles. They include, for example, rent and taxes on the premises; cost of services such as lighting, heating, telephone and insurance etc.

* Variable costs (also known as direct costs) are costs that vary according to production. They are costs that directly relate to the products you make. They include, for example, materials like wax and wick for production. Variable costs can be split into *material costs* and *labour costs,* but only count the labour that is used directly in candle production.

Some costs may seem to fit neither category exactly. For example, it is likely that there will be a standing charge for having electricity supplied to the premises, which is undoubtedly a fixed cost, but the amount of electricity used for production will vary with volume of candles made and is therefore a variable cost.

Income

Using the information you have gathered in stage one of the feasibility study, and having considered how you will build capacity to meet demand over time, you should be able to estimate some sales targets. Completing a series of tables like the one below will help to give you an overall picture of potential income from sales to different customer categories.

When you have a clear estimation of capital costs, income and expenditure for your first two or three years of business, you can begin to forecast the money you will spend and the money you will receive from the business. This is known as your cash flow. If at any stage you expect to need more money than you have

Table 2.1 Example three-year sales forecast for product A

	Showroom sales	Website sales	Craft fair sales	Total annual sales (pieces)	Sale value per piece (product A)	Total annual sales income
Year 1	1,000	0	0	1,000	10	10,000
Year 2	1,400	800	600	2,800	10.5	29,400
Year 3	1,800	2,200	1000	5,000	11	55,000

available, you will need to find additional finance. The feasibility study can include initial research into sources of finance that might be available to you, such as:

- Loans from individuals (e.g. family), credit organizations (e.g. micro-finance) or banks.
- Grants from business support organizations (e.g. local government schemes).
- Bank overdrafts (e.g. for short-term loans to avoid cash flow problems).

Analysis and interpretation of data

When the results of the feasibility study have been organized and collated you can begin to make some informed decisions about the potential viability of the business idea. With particular reference to the information about income and expenditure that you have brought together in the final section of your feasibility study, you will need to assess whether or not your proposed candle-making enterprise is in fact a sound business idea. Is there a real demand? Is it sufficiently profitable? What is the level of risk? Is this manageable for you? Should you go ahead and invest in the business? To help answer these questions it is useful to develop a SWOT (strengths, weaknesses, opportunities and threats) analysis in relation to your business. An example SWOT analysis is shown in Figure 3.1.

If you do decide to take your business idea forward, the next step is to build upon the information in your feasibility study and develop a more detailed business plan.

CHAPTER 3

Business planning

with contributions from Mindy Chillery

What is a business plan?

A business plan is a written document that draws together a wealth of information about your business. Even if you intend to start very small, a simple written business plan will help you to reduce the chances of wasting time and money. Your business plan should allow someone who has no previous knowledge of your business to become fully informed about your vision and targets. They should get an understanding of the type and size of the business and how it will operate on a practical and financial level. The plan should also explain how your own skills and experience fit the business idea. A good deal of the information you require will be gained from your initial feasibility study, but there will also be some work to do to increase the detail, and you should be prepared to do further research in areas where there are gaps or topics that you are unsure about.

Why have a business plan?

A business plan is often required by banks or other organizations that offer investment or loans to your business, or perhaps other forms of enterprise development support such as training, or specific business advice. However a business plan is also an essential document for you to use yourself. It allows you to properly think through all the important elements of your enterprise, and the process of writing the plan to a standard structure will often help you identify weaknesses and gaps in your thinking. It will also form a good point of reference from which you can articulate your ideas to other people. In the future you can look back at your original business plans and evaluate your level of success, compared to your predictions. It is good practice to regularly up-date and adapt the plan according to how the business progresses. This will help you to stay on track towards your original vision and ensure that any adjustments you make do not undermine the achievement of your overall goals.

A business plan will help you to:

- identify priorities and avoid being distracted from them;
- be clear and realistic about your goals;
- manage your time effectively;
- manage your finances effectively;
- identify potential risks and ways of avoiding or mitigating them;
- develop a long-term vision for your enterprise;
- communicate the potential of your business more effectively to key people (for example to potential investors).

Business plan structure

A suggested structure for a business plan is shown below. Try to keep the document simple whilst at the same time including all the essential information and do not make it any longer than necessary. Only include relevant information and keep to the point, avoiding elaborate language or jargon.

Section 1: Introductory details

1.1 State the business name and contact details.
1.2 How did the business idea originate and what is the motivation behind it?
1.3 A summary description of the size and nature of the proposed candlemaking business.
1.4 A brief overview of yourself and others involved in the enterprise. State how your experience and skills are relevant.

Section 2: Operating details

These will vary depending upon your country of operation.

2.1 State the ownership and legal structure of the business. For example do you intend to operate as a sole trader, a partnership, a limited company or a co-operative etc? Give the reason for the structure you have chosen and say what registrations or licences you require.

2.2 Show that you have properly considered the appropriate regulations concerning areas like health and safety, and environmental law.

2.3 Say what insurance your business requires. This will usually include public and product liability insurance and insurance to safeguard your staff at work.

Section 3: Market analysis

3.1 Describe the products you intend to produce and show that you have researched and know the type and size of the market for them. Explain the exact part of the market you intend to target and show that you know your potential customers and their reactions to your products.

3.2 Describe in detail how you will reach the market (e.g. by supplying shops, selling from your own shop or selling online) and what distribution channels will be used.

3.3 If you are planning new products, describe your ideas and the time frames involved. Say if you will use any outside services to assist with marketing.

3.4 Include information about your competitors. Who are your direct competitors and how do you intend to compete with them? Most of this section will come from your feasibility study and marketing plan (see Chapters two and four).

Section 4: Finance, including pricing, profit and loss and cash flow forecasts

4.1 Demonstrate that you have costed your products accurately, and you know the sale prices and profit margin. Use information from the feasibility study and your marketing plan, (see Chapter four for more information about pricing).

4.2 Include a monthly profit and loss forecast for the first year (including start-up costs) and a quarterly forecast for year two. This must show money you expect to receive (from your sales forecast) and money you expect to go out of the business, including all variable and fixed costs. The objective is to calculate your estimated net (total) profit or loss month by month. Potential investors will require your forecasts to be realistic and convincing if they are going to make money available to you.

4.3 Your cash flow forecast should also be properly calculated and show the months in which money is expected to come into, and go out of the business. This will show if and when the business will need to borrow money to allow trading to continue. Again potential investors will need to be sure that your enterprise does not plan to expand too fast for the cash available (known as over trading).

4.4 Explain your funding sources (for example your own money, grants, loans, bank overdraft facilities). Provide an overview of your personal finances demonstrating how you will manage financially in the period that the business plan is covering. Again, if you are using the business plan to apply for investment in your enterprise you will need to be clear and specific about exactly what you require. Potential investors will want to know how their funds will fit into the financial forecasts you have made.

Section 5: Production

5.1   Briefly explain what production facilities are necessary to achieve the volume and quality of products required.

5.2   Explain what materials and consumables are required and show that you have identified reliable suppliers.

5.3   Say what premises has been identified and why it is suitable in terms of services, security and length of lease etc. Is the size adequate for any planned growth?

5.4   State any unique or unusual aspects to your production processes as compared to your competitors, and explain any plans to develop your production techniques.

Section 6: SWOT analysis and risk log

Consider including a SWOT analysis and risk log in your business plan. A SWOT analysis is a simple method by which to consider the strengths, weaknesses, opportunities and threats (SWOT) of your business. You could also analyse at least one of your competitors (see Figure 3.1).

Strengths	Weaknesses
Original unique designs	Limited production capacity
Good technical know-how	Inexperienced in marketing and promotion
Personalized customer service	Limited funds to support development
IT skills of staff	

Opportunities	Threats
Development of website and cost-effective e-marketing	Possible illness of key staff and impact on production and development
Small business allowing quick development of new innovative designs for new markets	Unexpected increases in material costs

Figure 3.1 Example SWOT analysis

The production of a risk log will show that you have thought through any potential risks to the new enterprise. Show that you have identified actions that will help to prevent risks that are likely to have a high or medium impact and also have a high or medium risk of occurring. In the example in Figure 3.2, risks one and three are deemed high impact with a medium likelihood of occurring. It is, therefore, more important to consider how such eventualities can be avoided than spending time on avoiding risk two, which in this case is deemed to have only a low chance of occurring.

	Probability of risk occurring			Probable impact		
Risk 1	Low	Medium	High	Low	Medium	High
Sales targets not achieved		Y				Y
Any action to be taken to mitigate risk	Review marketing plan quarterly to ensure marketing activities are effective and adjust as necessary. Review product range every six months and adjust to meet demand.					
	Probability of risk occurring			Probable impact		
Risk 2	Low	Medium	High	Low	Medium	High
High number of customers don't pay	Y					Y
Any action to be taken to mitigate risk	Set systems in place to ensure payment is received before delivery					
	Probability of risk occurring			Probable impact		
Risk 3	Low	Medium	High	Low	Medium	High
Raw materials not delivered on time		Y				Y
Any action to be taken to mitigate risk	Ensure orders for raw materials are made in good time Ensure orders are made and confirmed in writing Try out new suppliers at less busy times of the year					

Figure 3.2 Example risk log

Section 7: Appendix

You may wish to include an appendix section at the end of your business plan. This might contain your key research data, references, and other information that is important but too detailed to be included in the body of the business plan text.

Using your business plan

Once your business plan is written, ask other entrepreneurs to read it and give you critical feedback. When you are happy with the content, you can use it for your own planning and if necessary present it to potential investors. However, do not regard the document as a finished masterpiece. Remember its content is based largely on estimates and predictions, and the reality may prove to be quite different. As your business develops you will become well placed to review and up-date your future plans in the light of your real-life business experiences.

CHAPTER 4

Marketing

with contributions from Mindy Chillery

Marketing is one of the most important areas of activity for any small business. If you want to grow and ensure that your business is strong enough to survive, you cannot afford to overlook the vital, long-term role that marketing plays. It is sometimes easy to be tempted into spending large sums of money on untested marketing activities, but this is not usually necessary. There are many positive and constructive things that you can do to promote your business that will only require energy and creativity, with very little outlay. When you are starting your business, this is usually the most sensible approach. As you begin to understand your customers and market more, you can decide if greater financial investment is needed and, if so, what will be the most effective activities.

This chapter looks at the four elements of marketing in turn, with particular detail on pricing your products. It also includes advice on developing a marketing plan and setting targets.

What is marketing?

Marketing is made up of four elements. They are commonly referred to as *the four Ps: Product, Price, Place and Promotion.*

This means that successful marketing requires:

- *Product.* Offering a product that the market wants. Making the product appropriate to the market segment you are trying to sell into.
- *Price.* Selling the product at a price that the market will accept. It is particularly important to know how your price compares to your competitors.

- *Place.* Making the product accessible to the market. Where will your customers come into contact with your products and be able to buy them?
- *Promotion.* Bringing the product effectively to the market's attention.

The four P's can be summarized by saying that successful marketing requires knowledge of the market into which you want to sell your product, and the capacity to respond to it. As a candlemaker you need to know who your customers are; what type and quality of candles they want; what they are prepared to pay; what sort of service they expect; and where they will go to buy your candles. Marketing is often also described as an attitude of mind. Any producer or trading organization will be constantly reviewing the products they offer, and how and where they sell them. This can be represented as a circular process as shown in the diagram below:

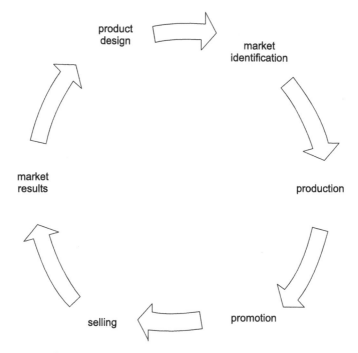

Figure 4.1 Marketing process

Product: Knowing what your customers want

Getting the product right is particularly critical to the success of a small-scale candlemaking business. The issues associated with design and production of your products, are examined in Chapters five and seven. However when thinking about your product from a marketing perspective, you should be aware that the service you provide your customers, is also part of your product. You have already identified some ideal customers as part of your feasibility study. Try to expand your understanding by further consultation with your customer groups and more detailed research into the products and services they require. Regularly review the profile of your ideal customers as part of your marketing and business planning process and gradually strengthen this information as your business develops.

Your customers' inclination to do business with you rather than a competitor will be influenced by a number of factors, not just product and price. Customers may be attracted to other aspects of your service such as providing a fast turn around to enquiries and good friendly communication. As a small business you may be able to offer a personal touch, which bigger companies cannot. However ensure that you are also professional and reliable at all times, as it is essential to build customer confidence. You might find that customers value these services highly enough to pay a premium in price. Alternatively, you may be offering a particular service that your customers do not particularly value and find they would rather pay less for the product and forgo the unnecessary service. Periodically you should review all aspects of your overall offering. Consider what changes you might make to your products, service and to the overall customer experience. To help think this through try imagining that you have no time or money barriers that may constrain your ideas. This will allow you to think creatively and you may be able to implement some small changes immediately. If not, it is at least useful to record your ideas for reference when reviewing your products and services in the future.

Price and calculating costs

Pricing is one of the most difficult yet crucial aspects of running a small-scale craft business, as there are many factors to consider. First of all you have to be sure that you really know all the costs you incur in making, promoting and selling your products. If you underestimate these costs your business will be in trouble from the very start. You also have to decide what level of profit you require and this must then be added onto your costs. Once the total costs are accurately calculated you will need to identify the price that you think the market will bear. This is perhaps the most difficult task because it is mostly based on the subjective views of your potential customers and comparisons with the products of your competitors.

Once your costs are accurately calculated and your retail price is chosen, you will be able to see if the product is financially viable. If your total costs are higher than the selling price you will of course have to think again. However if all your costs and profit add up to less than your sale price, you have a viable starting point.

To ensure that you can calculate the true costs involved in producing your products, you should first understand the difference between 'variable costs', 'fixed costs' and 'profit'.

Variable costs (also known as direct costs)

These are made up of all the costs that you incur as a result of *actually making* the candles and any associated accessories and packaging. Typically these will include the cost of production materials such as wax, wick, dye, and product packaging etc. Also included in variable costs will be labour that is used directly in making or packing the product, and other costs that vary with the amount of candles made, such as the cost of fuel to melt the wax.

Fixed costs (also known as overheads or indirect costs)

These are costs that you incur as a result of operating your business, regardless of how many candles you produce. They include costs such as rent, insurance, labour for general business management and administration such as accounting etc.

Profit

This is the money the business earns from sales once the variable and fixed costs have been paid.

Selling overheads

It is necessary to understand your various selling overheads as they are often neglected. These are the costs associated with each market type that you sell your candles into. For example, you may sell your candles in three ways: from a website, at a craft market stall and through orders from a trade exhibition. You will therefore have a different set of selling overheads for each of your three markets. The website selling overheads would include things like the hosting of the site, the cost of website design and development, and the costs of maintaining and promoting the site. The market stall would include the cost of hiring the stall, travel and accommodation costs, and the cost of labour to staff the stall and organize the event. Similarly, the selling overheads for a trade fair will include the cost of hiring the exhibition space, cost of any printed leaflets or posters, and, as with the market stall, cost of travel, accommodation and staffing.

To be sure that you have a high enough selling price for your product in each market area the following simple sum can be used:

variable costs + fixed costs + selling overhead + profit = minimum price

Labour

With respect to the cost of labour, even if you are making the majority of the candles yourself and staffing your own events, you should always factor wages into the costing. You may find it useful to consider an hourly rate that you would be happy to pay (or to work for yourself). Alternatively, you might approach labour costs by considering how much you would realistically like to earn in a year, then divide this by the number of weeks you intend to work, and then by the number of hours to give you an hourly rate. When initially assessing your production costs you will need to record how long it takes to make each candle (or batch of candles) and calculate the associated labour costs.

For example, if you pay two people £8 an hour (for an 8 hour day) the labour cost per day is:

$$2 \text{ people} \times 8\text{hrs} \times £8 = £128$$

To make and pack 640 candles in a day, the cost of labour per candle is:

$$\text{labour cost } £128 \div 640 \text{ candles} = £0.20$$

Knowing the time taken and the cost of labour to make each of your products is extremely important to ensure you can accurately cost your products, and therefore plan your work programme and meet your production commitments.

Incorporating fixed costs

One important aspect of product pricing is to ensure that the fixed costs (overheads) of your whole business are properly covered within your product costing calculations. To do this you will need to take your total fixed costs for one year and divide this figure by the total number of hours that the business operates in a year. This gives you an hourly fixed costs rate, which you can then apply to all your candle costings. Apply the same method to the fixed costs specific to each of your markets (e.g. website, market stall, trade sales) in order to calculate an additional selling overhead rate appropriate for each market.

The following example illustrates the method:

Adam starts up a candle making business. He designs a new highly ornamental candle and needs to know how much it will cost to produce. To do this he lists the materials required for each candle and works out the material costs. Then he adds in the labour (his time in making the candles). Adam decides to pay himself £10 per hour and finds he can make four candles per hour. This means the labour cost for each candle is £2.50 (£10 ÷ 4).

Table 4.2 Variable costs for Adam's candle

Cost item	£'s
Labour	2.50
Wax	0.20
Wick	0.05
Dye	0.05
Packaging	1.00
Total cost	£3.80

Adam now has to incorporate his annual fixed costs (rent, taxes, electricity, general admin, pension etc.) into the candle costing. He calculates that his total fixed costs are £2,000 a year. He works 45 weeks of the year for 37 hours a week. This means he has an hourly fixed costs rate of:

$$£2,000 \div 45 \text{ (weeks)} \div 37 \text{ (hours)} = £1.20$$

Because he makes four candles an hour, his fixed costs per candle are £0.30 (£1.20 ÷ 4)

Adam now knows his variable costs per candle and his fixed costs per candle. Next he has to work out his selling overheads. Adam intends to sell the candles in three ways: through his website, at a market stall and at an annual trade exhibition. He calculates that:

- The website costs associated with selling this design are £200
- The market stall costs associated with selling this design are £450
- The trade exhibition costs associated with selling this design are £150

He goes on to estimate that he can sell 100 of the candles a year through the website, 200 a year through the market stall and 1,000 a year through the trade exhibition.

His selling overheads are therefore:

- Website costs £200 ÷ 100 (candles) = £2.00 per candle
- Market stall costs £450 ÷ 200 (candles) = £2.25 per candle
- Trade exhibition costs £150 ÷ 1,000 (candles) = £0.15 per candle

Putting all this information together in Table 4.3 Adam can see clearly the costs involved in each of the three different ways of selling.

Table 4.3 Costs and pricing for Adam's candle

	Variable costs per candle	Fixed costs per candle	Selling overhead per candle	Total cost of candle	Retail price per candle	Profit per candle	Trade price per candle	Total profit
100 website sales (100 pieces)	3.80	0.30	2.00	6.10	10.00	3.90	–	390.00
Market stall sales (200 pieces)	3.80	0.30	2.25	6.35	10.00	3.65	–	730.00
Trade exhibition sales (1,000 pieces)	3.80	0.30	0.15	4.25	–	0.75	5.00	750.00

Trade pricing for retailers

If you are selling to retailers in order for them to sell your products to the final customer, you should expect the retailer to mark-up your product, usually by at least 100 per cent. This is sometimes called the *margin* and covers the retailer's own profit and fixed costs, such as the rent, staffing and marketing of their shop. You must, therefore, be sure that if you want to enter the trade market, it is still viable for you to sell your product to retailers (your trade customers) for much less than the final retail selling price (usually 50 per cent or less). It is also important to bear in mind that your final retail price should be reasonably consistent, whatever market you are selling through. For example, a retailer would be dissatisfied if they found that you were selling your products at a lower price through your website than the retail price you have recommended to them. You can therefore suggest a recommended retail price (RRT) to your trade customers.

Pricing summary

It is important that the price of the candle includes some margin for profit to enable you to invest further in the business and eventually increase your earnings. In general the bigger the difference between the costs and the selling price the better (i.e. the bigger the profit). However if the selling price is set too high it will have the effect of reducing the number of sales, and your sales targets will not be reached. The *art* of pricing, therefore, is to maximize your selling price without setting the price so high that it adversely effects the number of sales. The *science* of pricing is to accurately calculate all costs, and to ensure that the product price and sales volumes cover those costs and include sufficient profit. This does not mean that all products need to make the same amount of profit. You may offer a low-priced product that will 'hook' customers in. They may then buy higher priced products from your range once they have learnt to trust and rely on you to meet and even exceed their expectations.

Placement: Market penetration

Once you have a good idea of your potential customers and your overall offering, you can start to consider your 'routes to market'. Keep an open mind, ask friends to assist you to build business contacts, and get involved with local networking groups. There are also various formal organizations that may help introduce you to customers, such as retail and small business associations, and Chambers of Commerce etc. You will need to prioritize which marketing activities to undertake. For example, advertising in national or local magazines, developing and marketing a website, showing your candles at exhibitions and trade shows, direct mailing, local and national craft markets etc. Some candle-makers organize parties at friends and acquaintances homes. Some companies even hold virtual candle parties online which can reach an international audience.

Although you will not want to spread yourself too thinly, it is useful to have a mix of marketing tactics, so that you can get a feel for which is the most effective. When choosing which activities to prioritize, consider the following:

- How will the activity help you to reach your target customers?
- How will it enable you to communicate the benefits of your products?

- How much it is going to cost you and what return will you need to make it worthwhile?
- How can you enhance the impact of the activity by linking it with other activities or actions you are taking?

It is important that you allocate adequate time to your marketing activities, including time for preparation, planning and follow-up. Ensure you are clear about how you will measure the effectiveness of the particular activity. How will you know if it has actually brought you new business? Plan regular times to review your marketing actions (e.g. quarterly) so that you can assess what is working and what is not, as you go along.

Common selling opportunities

This section offers more detailed advice and tips about three means of selling that are commonly used by small-scale candle producers, namely, crafts fairs, trade fairs and from a website.

Craft fairs: Many candlemakers start off by participating in craft fairs or small street markets. This is a cost effective way to get your products exposed to potential customers, and to allow you to directly gauge their reaction and feedback. Some candlemakers continue to sell through craft fairs over many years, and become adept at selecting the best events to attend. Fair organizers will make a rental charge for a stall (or pitch) at their events, and these costs can vary dramatically. At the simplest level you may be offered a table at a school or church fair, and the charges may be minimal. However, remember that many small traders have experienced the feeling of wasted hours at poorly attended craft fairs and wishing they had never accepted the offer. The trick is to be selective, talk to people who have experience of fairs and other market stall-holders and find out which are the busy and well-attended events. If there is competition to get a place at a fair, and a rigorous application process, you should not necessarily be put off because these factors suggest that the level of sales will be good. The stall rentals will also be higher for profitable fairs, reflecting the demand for space at the event. Do not underestimate the time and energy required to run a good stall. You will need to consider the following:

- *Space and facilities.* What do you get for your stall rental? Is it just a space in a field or a fully equipped indoor exhibition space or something in-between? What size is the space and how much counter/wall space do you have? Is electricity available? How will you display your products to their full advantage? What will you need to dress your stall? Think about display tables, backdrops, posters and signs etc.
- *Stock.* Estimating stock levels can be difficult for first time stall-holders. You will not want to make and transport excessive quantities of stock to the event, but neither will you want to run out. One way to estimate is to approximate the quantity of stock you would be very pleased to sell, and then take a bit more. If it is a multi-day or multi-week event you will need to plan for re-stocking as you go.
- *Transport and staffing.* If your products and equipment are bulky or heavy, how will they be transported, and who will unload and load when you are at the event? Do you have enough people to staff the stall, especially during busy selling periods? Is food and accommodation arranged?
- *Regulations and safety.* Check the specific requirements of the event organizers. Some events will require you to have public liability insurance and may stipulate some health and safety requirements such as electrical testing or a risk assessment.
- *Payments.* Do you have cash for giving customers change, and will you accept payment cards? If so, do you have the facilities to accept cards, or do you need to rent a portable card-processing machine?

Trade fairs: Selling through retailers can be advantageous for the small candlemaker because it means that you do not have to spend time and energy servicing large numbers of individual customers yourself. Instead your customers are the retail owners and managers often known as 'buyers'. The significant disadvantage however, is that buyers will expect you to sell your products to them at much lower prices than you would sell to end customers (see *trade pricing for retailers* section above). If you do plan to sell to buyers (also known as 'the trade') you can either approach shops individually or attend trade fairs and exhibitions which are designed specifically to allow manufacturers and wholesalers to offer their products to a range of retailers. These events are efficient because they allow you to meet a large number of potential retail customers in a short space of time. Trade fairs are expensive to attend, so do some research and choose the events that will be most suitable for your business. Make sure your ideal customers will be amongst the visitors. Look for trade fairs that have sections for your kind of products, perhaps a handmade crafts section, or an area for first time exhibitors.

Trade fairs are professional environments, so it is important that you have confidence in your business and are knowledgeable about your products and service, before exposing them to professional scrutiny. Unlike craft fairs you will not be selling directly from your trade fair stand, so will only need products for display and not as stock. Neither will you normally need cash or credit card payment facilities. However, you will need to consider the other points mentioned for craft fairs and make sure that your stand looks smart, clean and generally professional. Pay particular attention to lighting and a well-ordered product display. When talking to prospective trade customers be particularly well prepared in the following areas:

- *Product details.* Be ready to answer questions about your products, and take the opportunity to emphasize special features or unique characteristics. Know the range of colours, scents and sizes and talk about what end customers like about the products, and why they buy them. Draw attention to any 'point of sale' display materials you offer.
- *Prices and order forms.* Have a price list for customers and know the trade price and the recommended retail price (RRP) of each product. State any relevant taxes (e.g. VAT). Have a supply of order forms so that you can take orders efficiently.
- *Terms of sale.* Decide in advance if you want to impose a minimum order value. Also know if you will offer products on a sale or return (SOR) basis. Know any standard quantities that you package candles in (e.g. box of 24) and any volume discounts you offer.

- *Lead times.* Know your lead times. This is the time your customer should expect to wait between making an order and receiving delivery.
- *Leaflets and promotional literature.* It is important to have good quality accurate printed materials for customers to take away. This will be the only thing that represents your business to them after leaving your exhibition stand.
- *Collect contact details.* If a customer shows real interest in your products, but does not place an order there and then, ask them for their business card or contact details.

After attending a trade fair or visiting retailers always confirm orders in writing and make follow-up enquiries as appropriate.

You may decide to approach trade customers directly, rather than paying to participate in costly trade fairs. If so, try to identify the type of retail outlets most appropriate to your product range, and preferably those that are busy and will sell your product at a reasonable rate. Consider the important characteristics of the retail outlets you want to target. For example, if you have identified gift shops as a likely sales opportunity, see if you can narrow this down any further: gift shops in a particular area; gift shops selling a high proportion on local crafts; gift shops with a high visitor rate etc. Remember you are trying to identify customers that are most likely to respond positively to your specific products and the service you provide. Work towards identifying a shortlist of shops that you would like to target over the next twelve months. You can then focus your marketing efforts on securing these relationships so as to make progress against your sales forecast targets.

Website: Although it is beyond the scope of this book to offer detailed information about marketing and selling on the internet, it is important for any small business to have a clear plan concerning its online profile and activities. A lot of small entrepreneurs will immediately want to get started on producing their own website, whilst others will be less enthusiastic or even daunted by the prospect. First of all it is important to know what you are trying to achieve by developing your internet presence. Key to this is the question: is online selling a part of your business plan? If the answer is no, then you may not need a website at all, or it may be better to set up a very simple website with introductory information about your business and how to contact you directly for more details. Many ISP (internet service providers) offer ready-made inexpensive packages that you can customize into a professional looking website for this purpose. However, if you do plan to make significant sales online you will need to have a better technical understanding of the issues. Unless you are already knowledgeable yourself, be prepared to enlist technical expertise, or to learn quickly. Even if you are not selling directly through your website, it may be useful to know how you can increase the number of potential customers who find it.

Getting a website up and running is only the first step. Like anything else in your business, your website will not work for you unless you put some careful thought into its design and promotion, and continue to develop it and keep it updated over time. There is plenty of advice and opinion concerning online marketing, and many professionals offering their services in this field. The points below are designed to give you a starting point as to how your business can begin to create a significant and expanding online presence:

- Keep your website up-to-date and put on new and interesting content as often as possible. You want returning customers to see something engaging so that they stay for a while.
- Build a community around your website by writing a blog, a newsletter, or setting up forums.
- You can find out the words most customers use when searching for products like yours by registering with major search engines and researching this subject. You then need to make sure that your website contains a good number of these (key) words. When executing a search, any search engine will be looking to find the sites that are most active and have the most repeated connection to the key words used in the search. Knowing what key words your potential customers use most will also help you if you decide to use a 'pay per click' service, such as Google Adwords.
- Maximize links to and from your site. Have a presence on important social networking sites and make links to your website. Register with online directories. All these things

increase the interactivity of your site and, therefore, your search engine optimization.

Advertising

Advertising online or in newspapers or magazines can be an effective way of bringing your products to the attention of potential customers, but some research is needed before you make any significant financial outlay for advertising space. As always, think first about your customers. In what particular media are they likely to see your advert? Publishing houses should be able to give you a profile of their readership and their circulation numbers. Make a shortlist of possible publications that you are going to advertise in and become familiar with them. Which adverts stand out to you and why? As with any promotional material, always ensure that your advert is attention grabbing and communicates your message clearly. It should also include an explicit instruction to the reader, for example, to buy from your website, or to call you with a discount code. The instruction should be easy and clear to carry out. If you are not a designer yourself, most publications will be happy to prepare the necessary artwork for you or alternatively you can enlist the services of a graphic designer or copywriter. Always remember to check artwork very carefully, particularly for correct spelling, especially the contact details such as telephone numbers and your website address. Always negotiate to ensure you obtain the best price for your advert. You will be in a strong position the first time you advertise in any particular publication or website as they will be hoping that after your first positive experience of advertising with them you will become a regular, long-term customer. If you are looking for discounted advertising space, find out the publication's print deadlines and call shortly before they go to print. If they have not reached their advertising income target, you will be well placed to negotiate a reduced price. You may also be able to negotiate other advantages such as: a bigger advert for the same price, an advert on their website or on a sister publication, or free advertising space in a future issue.

Also consider how you will know if a customer has come to you because of your advert. Perhaps your advert will include a special promotion, such as requiring the customer to quote the name of the publication to access a discount. In this way you can monitor the success of your advert and compare the effectiveness of the same advert in different publications.

As previously mentioned, you can use a search engine service (such as Google Adwords) to advertise online. In this sort of service you pay each time someone clicks on the advert which takes them through to your website (known as 'pay per click'). You will be able to choose what key words you want to use for a particular campaign and you will be given the opportunity to write the advert and to set a budget for your campaign. The budget you set will dictate the amount of times your advert appears when someone types in the particular key words you have chosen. Through your online service account you will be able to access useful information about your campaign, for example which key words brought you the most clicks.

Promotion: Attracting customer attention

Having developed a good picture of each group of your ideal customers, and identified what mix of marketing activities you are going to undertake to reach them, you need to take the next step and consider how you can promote your products to these people or organizations.

If you are showing your candles at an exhibition, trade fair or market, you may consider offering talks or demonstrations in addition to printed material. Some candlemakers open their workshops to visitors so that they can see how the candles are made and others do demonstrations in candlemaking at schools, festivals and other community gatherings. Competitions can also be a useful way of promoting interest in your products and gaining the contact details of potential customers. Special offers may encourage them to make a first purchase, providing you with the opportunity to build a longer-term relationship. Local press, particularly newspapers, magazines and radio are often a good way of promoting your marketing activities and, whatever activities you have decided to engage in, you will need at least some written promotional material and will probably want to write a press release from time to time. When preparing a press release consider the sort of information the media organization is interested in. Local press will generally be looking to keep their readers informed with up-to-date information about subjects of interest, local radio will often take a more informal angle and will be interested in stories that are controversial, quirky or funny. Local television will be similar, but particularly interested in stories that offer great picture opportunities. Stories might be things like a 'rags-to-riches' story about yourself, a charity event you are supporting, an interesting or unusual story about why you started your business, or an award you have won. Once you are sure you have a newsworthy event or story write the press release with an attention grabbing headline and make sure the text is short and sharp, usually no more than one side of paper. Ensure that your contact details are prominent on the press release. It is worth contacting the relevant media organization first to get an actual name to send the press release to. There will be someone whose specific job it is to decide what is 'news' and what is not. This person will decide whether or not to pass a press release on to an editor or journalist, or to reject it.

When you are producing any promotional material, whether it be for your stationery, website, email distributions, brochures, etc., you should stay true to your business branding. How do your materials communicate a strong business identity, which demonstrate the core values behind the company? Your logo is a particularly important tool in this respect. The public face of the business should appropriately reflect the quality and nature of your products and services at all times. If, for example, you are selling your candles as luxury handmade items of quality, it is important that a leaflet promoting the candles is also well designed and of high quality. You should also think about exactly how you will catch the attention of your target customers. What aspirations might they have that you could use as a theme or headline? If you are particularly targeting the gift market, for example, you might theme a leaflet along the lines of, 'unique Christmas gift', or 'the perfect Valentine gift'. You need also to communicate the qualities of the products that will enhance their life or their business, and build desire for it. How will you communicate your overall offering? You can build desire by including things like free gifts, special offers or no-risk guarantees. It is important to build urgency into your offer so always give a deadline. This also protects you from customers coming to you years later demanding you honour the offer when it is no longer part of your marketing activities! Finally, don't forget that it is important that your marketing materials have 'a call to action'. You need to explicitly ask your customers to buy and make it clear how they can do so. Try to make the process of buying as easy as possible.

Setting targets

Finally, your marketing plans should include annual sales targets. It is good to set sales targets that will stretch you a little, but it is also important that you have a justification for feeling that they are achievable. Avoid just plucking figures out of the air. Think about what information you have that will inform the targets you are setting (for example your feasibility study research). To begin with all your customers will be new, but gradually you will develop targets for existing markets as well. Targets should be expressed in specific numbers with a time scale, for example:

- In the next 12 months we aim to achieve a sales income of £5,000 from gift candles to individuals.
- In the next 12 months we aim to achieve a sales income of £3,000 from gift candles to retailers.

This can then be further broken down into quarterly or monthly sales targets.

Summary

Remember that people are at the heart of marketing and a successful business builds long-term trusting relationships. You are aiming to offer the customer a quality experience, not only in the product but also in the process of buying it. Whatever your approach, the aim is to get noticed, get remembered and to keep on expanding your customer base.

CHAPTER 5

Materials, equipment and techniques

This chapter explains the various production methods for candle-making and gives advice on selecting and using candlemaking materials and equipment. It also offers ideas for creative and decorative variations and starts with a technical explanation of how a candle actually works.

How a candle burns

Although a candle appears to be a very simple product, it is not commonly known how it actually works. When the wick of a candle is lit the heat of the flame begins to melt the surrounding fuel (wax) into a liquid pool; this liquid wax is then absorbed by the wick. The heat produced causes the liquid wax to vaporize and this vapour becomes the fuel for the burning flame. In a well designed candle the wick and the wax will burn off at a slow and uniform rate to provide a steady flame and dripping will not occur.

Candlemaking materials

Waxes, the fuel for the candle

Historically, candles were made from animal fats such as beef, sheep and whale fat, but today cleaner and more efficient waxes are used. Most modern handmade candles are made predominantly from paraffin wax, which is usually mixed with a small proportion of other high quality wax such as stearin. However a range of natural waxes are now becoming increasingly common and more popular.

Paraffin wax: Paraffin wax is the most important raw material used in candlemaking. It is available in solid slabs or as pellets or flakes. It is white in appearance but becomes clear when in liquid form, although it can be bought pre-dyed in a range of colours. It is odourless, tasteless and hard to the touch at room temperature. Paraffin waxes are supplied with various melting-points ranging from 46°C to 68°C. Those waxes which melt at around 58°C are ideal for candlemaking in temperate climates, although wax with a higher melting point is better for use in hotter climates. Most suppliers will offer a slightly lower price for paraffin wax in slab form but pellets or flakes are more convenient to weigh out and are generally easier to handle.

Stearin: Stearin (sometimes known as stearic acid) is a component of many animal and vegetable fats and has become an important material in candlemaking. It is important as a hardening agent for paraffin wax owing to its good temperature stability. It helps to overcome the problem of 'bending', which is sometimes experienced with paraffin wax candles in hotter climates. Stearin also helps in the release of candles from moulds and most importantly it considerably improves burning qualities when mixed with paraffin wax. It is commonly supplied as white flakes or granules. Stearin is usually added to paraffin wax in quantities of about 10 per cent but this can be increased to achieve quality improvements. Candles made from 100 per cent stearin are slow burning and non-drip, and have a crystalline appearance, which is appealing for some applications. The price of stearin is higher than paraffin wax.

Beeswax: Beeswax is a very highly regarded candlemaking material. It is excellent for making dipped and poured candles, which are usually marketed as a premium product. The wax burns slowly and tends to give off a pleasant natural aroma. Beeswax is obtained by melting the honeycomb in which bees store their honey. Once the honey is removed the comb is melted and usually cleaned by straining. At this stage it is a brownish-yellow colour but it can be lightened by bleaching or by extended exposure to sunlight. The wax has a melting point of about 64°C, and is a relatively soft and sticky substance which means it can be difficult to mould in rigid moulds. Beeswax can be mixed with paraffin wax in quantities of about 5–10 per cent to improve both the burning time and appearance of the candles. Candles made from pure beeswax remain highly regarded as a slow burning natural product.

Vegetable waxes: Many plants, shrubs and trees yield waxes that can be extracted and processed for use in the manufacture of candles. In some cases it may be possible to use these waxes as the main source of fuel for the candle; in others it may only be possible to use them in small quantities to improve the qualities of another wax. Some vegetable waxes, such as soya and rapeseed, are marketed as sustainable and healthy alternatives to paraffin wax because they are derived from renewable sources and often burn more cleanly than paraffin wax. Soya wax is produced from soya oil, and is becoming increasingly popular with candle consumers. The oil is extracted from solid soya beans by mechanical pressing or solvent extraction, and then further refined. It is then hydrogenated to make the solid wax. About 100kg of oil can be extracted from 600kg of beans and the remaining solid by-products can be used as animal feed. Pure soya wax has a soapy feel quite different to paraffin wax and is too soft to make into self-standing pillar candles without adding other ingredients. It is therefore commonly used for container candles and can be dyed and scented.

Gel wax: This substance is made from 95 per cent mineral oil, and 5 per cent polymer resin and is unlike any other candlemaking material. It is clear in appearance and soft (jelly like) to touch. It has a high melting point and does not set hard like other waxes. It can therefore only be used in containers and because it is clear, candles can be decorated with non-flammable embedded items within the body of the candle. An American company (Penreco) owns the patent for gel wax and it is supplied in low, medium and high densities. Gel wax requires very little dye for colouring, but can only be safely scented with scents that are properly compatible with mineral oil (see section on making container candles).

Other waxes and additives: A variety of specialist waxes and additives are available from specialist candlemaking suppliers but none of these are essential to begin with. They include:

- Dip and carve wax, which is soft enough to carve and model at low temperatures.
- Microcrystalline waxes, which can be added to paraffin wax to reduce or increase hardness.
- Over-dipping wax, which gives a high gloss coating to a candle.

Wick

The wick is a very important component of a candle and should be selected with care. Most modern wick is made from braided cotton strands (not cotton thread). A flat braid is adequate for most candles but square and round braided wick is also available for thicker candles or those made from specialist waxes. Some wicks also include a paper or wire stiffener, which helps when making container candles. Lead core wicks used to be used, but should now be avoided due to the poisonous fumes they produce. In countries with established candlemaking industries wicks can be ordered directly from wholesalers or craft suppliers. It is also possible to make wicks by hand if necessary, but this is only practical in countries where labour intensive enterprises are viable. When the wick is lit, the flame should radiate sufficient heat to melt a small pool of wax at the top of the candle. The liquid wax is then drawn up towards the flame by capillary action where it vaporizes and is burnt. When lit, a correctly proportioned wick will curl into the hottest (outer) part of the flame and burn away at its tip, to give a clean bright flame.

The basic principle in selecting a wick is: the larger diameter the candle, the wider the wick. If the wick used is too wide, it will create a large flame that melts the wax too fast causing dripping on the outer edge of the candle. Conversely, if the wick used is too narrow, the flame will be unable to generate enough heat to vaporize sufficient wax and will probably 'drown' in its own wax pool. Substances such as beeswax, which are viscous when

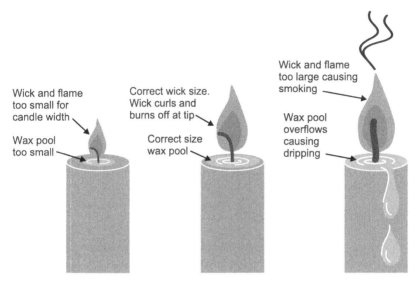

Figure 5.1 Wick selection

liquid, require a wider wick than substances with a lower viscosity. In general, the more viscous the liquid fuel, the wider the wick required. Some trial and error testing is usually necessary.

Dyes and scents

Where candles are being sold as decorative items rather than as a source of light, colour and scent are often used to increase the attractiveness of the product. Candle dyes are available in solid block form or as powder that can be directly added to the wax as it is melting. Wide ranges of colours are available and suppliers will provide information concerning quantities required, as this will vary depending upon the concentration of the dyes. It is advisable to mix small test samples of colour before producing candles, particularly since some colours tend to change as the wax cools. Some dyed candles will have a tendency to fade over time, especially if left in strong light.

Scented candles are now a well-established and popular product. Many countries have suppliers offering scents specifically designed for candles. These are liquids that are stirred into the melted wax during production. The result is a scented wax candle with a pleasant smell that will release more fragrance when it is lit. Some scents are specifically designed for use with natural waxes and others are better for paraffin based wax mixtures. The degree to which the scent is released from the wax is known as the 'throw'. Essential oils can be used as scents for candles and other locally available natural fragrances can be experimented with. Be sure to test burn candles with unconventional scents as some substances can smell bitter when burnt, or even cause flaring of the candle flame or other safety hazards.

Selecting material suppliers

Selecting suppliers is an important task for new businesses, and it is worth investing some time in making sure you are identifying the best suppliers for your business needs. You should ask potential suppliers not only about the products and prices they offer, but also their associated services. For example: what are their delivery times and charges? Do they have a minimum order value? How and when do they require payment? What is their returns policy for wrong or faulty goods? Also remember that the customer/ supplier relationship is two-way. It is useful to build a good rapport with your suppliers by conducting your business with them in a professional and friendly manner. Try not to make unreasonable demands and ensure that you pay invoices on time. If you are seen as a good customer, you are more likely to get good service, good prices and better credit terms. It is also handy to keep a list of possible alternative suppliers in case your existing ones run out of stock, or let you down at a critical time.

Some candlemaking suppliers are principally targeting the hobby market. These art and craft type suppliers usually hold a large range of materials and equipment, but in relatively small quantities. In general the larger quantity of materials you order, the better prices you will achieve. Some suppliers cater for larger volumes and hold large stocks of good quality materials that can be dispatched quickly. These are the suppliers most appropriate for candlemaking businesses, and this is particularly true when buying your wax, which is usually supplied in multiples of 20 or

25kg bags. You may decide, therefore, to buy from a variety of specialist suppliers, rather than trying to order everything from one company.

Candlemaking equipment

Heating methods

When heating wax it is very important to be aware of some essential safety precautions. It is imperative that wax is not overheated. At high temperatures (usually above about 150°C) wax will start to smoke and give off unpleasant and dangerous fumes. At a higher temperature wax will reach its 'flash point'. This is extremely dangerous because at these temperatures wax can spontaneously ignite. An open flame can also ignite very hot liquid wax. Once burning, liquid wax is difficult to extinguish and can cause a serious fire. If a fire does start, the heat source should be turned off immediately and if possible the burning wax should be starved of air (oxygen) by covering with a metal lid or fire blanket. On no account try to move a pan of overheated or burning wax and do not try to extinguish burning wax with water, as it will intensify the fire. The chances of overheating can be greatly reduced if the

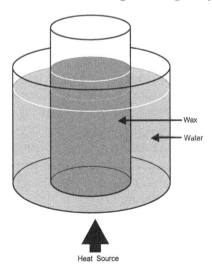

Wax

Water

Heat Source

Figure 5.2 Double boiler

wax melting pot is not heated directly. To do this, the melting pot can be placed into a larger container of hot water and the wax heated by the surrounding water. This is known as a double boiler (Figure 5.2). Although this is a relatively safe method of heating wax, you must always make sure that the water does not boil away, otherwise the wax will quickly overheat.

Electricity: Electricity is ideal as a source of heat as it is easily controlled. An ordinary domestic cooker can be used for heating fairly small quantities of wax. Alternatively a suitably sized tank can be fitted with electric heating elements at the bottom to make a custom designed melting tank. Purpose-built professional wax melters are also available from specialist suppliers. These are usually electrically powered and have an internal heating element and a thermostat that can be set to accurately control and maintain the wax temperature without the need for frequent manual checking and adjustment. There are a variety of designs on the market; some incorporate an integral double boiler system whilst others melt the wax directly. Sizes range from small table-top models to very large floor standing versions.

Gas: Gas is the most commonfuel used for wax melting. Domestic gas cookers can be used (a double boiler system is safest). If larger quantities of wax are required, purpose made equipment can be bought, but this can be expensive for small-scale production. Some candlemakers look for alternative equipment that has been designed for other applications, but can be improvised for candle-making purposes. One example of this is the use of bitumen (road tar) heating equipment used for wax instead of tar. If heating a container of wax directly, ensure that the container has a thick bottom to prevent the wax from burning and take careful precautions against hot wax coming into contact with the gas flame. The use of a heated water jacket will help to maintain the wax at a constant temperature.

Solid fuel: Solid fuel such as coal or firewood should only be used in situations where no other source of fuel is available. This is because it is difficult to control the heat levels and the open flame represents a fire risk. Great care must be taken to prevent wax from being spilt onto an open fire.

Containers for heating wax: Although there are containers specifically designed for candlemaking, many ordinary domestic or catering pots and pans are quite adequate to get started. Containers made of aluminum or stainless steel are ideal as they will not rust. However steel or iron can also be used, except in the case of beeswax, where iron equipment is not suitable. Copper and brass should be avoided as they cause oxidization.

Measuring and controlling temperature: The simplest means of measuring the temperature of melting wax is by the use of a cooking thermometer. A cooking thermometer (otherwise known as a 'jam' or 'sugar' thermometer) is ideal as it is reasonably accurate and will easily cope with the temperatures involved. It is important that a thermometer is not heated beyond its upper limit, as this will make it inaccurate in the future. If available, thermostatically controlled equipment such as the wax melters mentioned above are a very good means of setting and maintaining the temperature of the wax.

Production techniques

There are four basic methods of candlemaking (each described below) that are particularly suitable for small-scale manufacture:

- dipping;
- pouring;
- moulding (or casting);
- container candles.

Dipping

Dipping is the simplest method of making candles. It can be used to make a small number of candles by hand, with very simple equipment, or as a production process for manufacturing large numbers of candles in a variety of sizes and colours.

To dip candles, first heat the wax in a deep container to the required temperature. The temperature will vary according to the type of wax used, but 70°C is a good starting point (e.g. for 90 per cent paraffin wax to 10 per cent stearin). The appropriate thickness wick is then selected and lowered into the wax for the first time. For the first dip only, the wicks should be left to soak in the wax for about two minutes to allow air and moisture to escape. This process is known as 'priming the wicks' and should be done with all new wicks. The primed wicks can be drawn through the fingers as they cool, to straighten them and to remove any lumps. This will help to ensure that the finished candles are smooth and uniform. Once the wicks are primed the continual dipping process can begin. The wicks are repeatedly dipped into the hot wax for about 3–4 seconds at a time. They must be allowed to cool slightly between each dip (for between 1–4 minutes, depending upon room temperature). Each time the wicks are dipped another layer of wax is built up and the candles begin to take shape. In order to obtain a well-formed candle, it should be submerged and withdrawn reasonably quickly and as smoothly as possible to achieve even layers with no surface imperfections. A standard

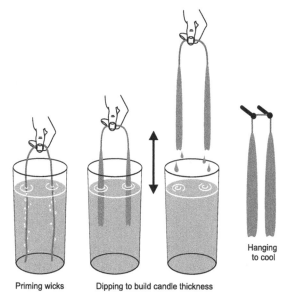

Priming wicks   Dipping to build candle thickness

Hanging to cool

Figure 5.3 Dipping by hand

dinner candle will require about 12 dips, depending upon the conditions. The length of the candles will result from the depth to which they are dipped and their thickness will be determined by the number of times they are dipped. The temperature of the liquid wax is important and should be continuously monitored. If the liquid wax becomes too hot it will melt off more wax from the candles than it adds. On the other hand, if the liquid wax is allowed to get too cool a fine skin will form on the top of the wax and interfere with the clean dipping process. The rate at which the candles grow depends upon three things: the temperature of the wax, the room temperature, and the time allowed between dips. When the required thickness has been achieved, the candles are removed, trimmed at their lower ends and allowed to cool.

Colours and effects: Dipped candles can be made from pre-coloured wax, which will give them a solid colour throughout their thickness. Alternatively they can be made in white wax and then given a few final dips in coloured wax, which will produce a coloured 'outer skin'. This is known as 'over-dipping' and requires wax that is strongly dyed to cover the inner candle. Professional over-dipping wax is also available from specialist suppliers.

The shape of dipped candles can be altered after the final dip and while the wax is still warm enough to manipulate without cracking. They can, for example be shaped into curves, twisted together or rolled flat and twisted, before being allowed to cool completely. Alternatively warm candles may be rolled on a flat glass or metal surface to achieve a very smooth surface finish.

Carving dipped candles: This is a specialist art-form which produces very decorative and elaborate candles. They are usually sold more as crafted ornaments rather than as candles for burning. For this process a moulded candle is dipped in a series of different colours, so as to create a variety of coloured layers that can be exposed as stripes when cut. Immediately after the dipping is complete the candle will remain warm and pliable for several minutes. During this period the candle is easily sliced through the outer layers using a sharp knife or carving tools. The resulting 'flaps' can then be curled or looped to expose the various decorative colours underneath. The carver must work fairly quickly, so as to complete the carving before the wax hardens. Once the carving is finished the candle is dipped in a coating of carvers glaze wax, which creates a tough glossy outer layer to protect the candle from damage and dust.

Dipping equipment: At the simplest level dipping may be carried out by holding the centre of a wick and dipping it repeatedly by hand, so that a pair of candles is produced (Figure 5.3). Although this will result in a low production rate, it is the principle on which all dipping equipment is based. In large-scale production, a large number of wicks are suspended from a frame and dipped in turn.

Figure 5.4 illustrates a continuous dipping process for four or more wick holders suspended from a wheel. Using this method, the wheel is rotated after each dip to enable a fresh set of wicks to be presented for dipping. Simple dipping frames of any configuration can be made to suit the size and shape of your dipping containers.

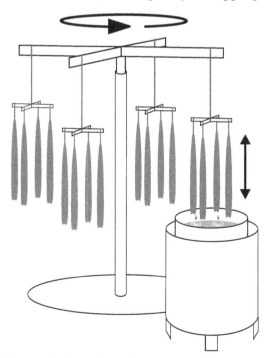

Figure 5.4 Continuous dipping equipment

Pouring

Pouring candles is very simple and similar in principle to dipping, as it is also a process that builds up candles layer by layer. However pouring is slower than dipping as only one candle can be poured at a time. For this reason it is normally only used for very small-scale production where a minimum of equipment is available.

To pour candles, wicks must first be primed (see section on dipping) and straightened. Wax is heated to the correct temperature (about 65–70°C depending upon wax type) and is poured down each wick in turn, using a jug or ladle. A container is positioned under the wick to catch the excess wax, which drips from the wicks. During pouring, the wick should be twisted slowly to aid the formation of an even coating of wax. It is only possible for a certain amount of wax to be added at each pouring. The candle must, therefore, be built up from many thin layers, the process being repeated until the required thickness has been achieved. It is important that the conditions are right for pouring, if the candles are too warm and/or the wax is too hot, the poured wax will tend to melt the previous layer. The temperature of the wax should, therefore, be adjusted to take into account the speed of

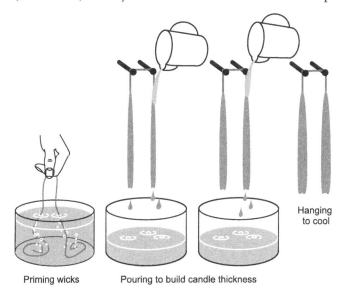

Priming wicks   Pouring to build candle thickness   Hanging to cool

Figure 5.5 Hand pouring

working, the workshop temperature and the composition of the wax mixture. Avoid hanging the candles too closely together as this may cause them to stick together as they sway during pouring. When a sufficient thickness of wax has been built up, the candles are left to set hard.

Colours and effects: When poured candles are still warm they can be shaped and rolled in a similar way to dipped candles (see previous section). They can be poured using solid colour or given a coloured finishing coat. Creative decorative effects are possible by experimenting with pouring multiple colours over finished candles.

Pouring equipment: The equipment used in the pouring process can be very simple (see Figure 5.6). In this example a bicycle wheel is supported horizontally at a suitable height, so that it can rotate freely. Wire hooks are fixed to the outer rim of the wheel, from

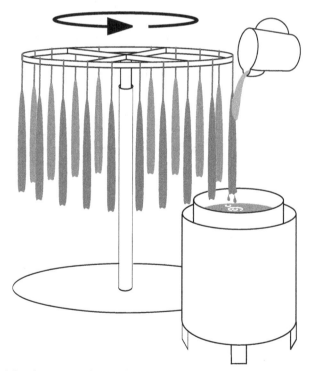

Figure 5.6 Continuous pouring equipment

which the candle wicks are suspended. Pre-heated wax is then poured over each wick and the excess wax is caught in a container below. After each pouring, the wheel is turned until the next wick is positioned above the wax container and the process is repeated until all the candles are of the required thickness.

Moulding (casting)

Candle moulding (or casting) is a method commonly used to make decorative and unusually shaped candles. Each candle produced will need time to cool in its mould, and this can be a limiting factor for large volume production, unless a large number of moulds are acquired. Candles can be moulded from a variety of wax types. Most commonly they are made from a mix of paraffin wax and stearin. The ideal wax will be a hard paraffin wax (with a melting point of about 60–68°C). This is less likely to stick to the sides of the mould than a softer, lower melting point wax. A relatively high proportion of stearin may be added to improve both the hardness of the candle and its shrinkage when cooling, thus aiding the removal of the candle from the mould.

While the wax is melting the mould can be prepared. A wick of suitable thickness should be primed (see section on dipping) and threaded through the hole in the mould (there is usually a hole in the bottom of the mould for this purpose). Seal the hole with mould sealant (available from candlemaking suppliers) or an equivalent substance. Tie the other end of the wick to a thin stick or rod and ensure the wick is taut and centrally positioned. When the temperature of the wax is about 90°C use a jug to carefully pour the wax into the centre of the mould. Try to fill the mould at a slow but continuous rate, without splashing or pouring onto the sides of the mould. After a minute or two give the mould a tap to dislodge any trapped air. Now the candle can be left to harden or placed in a water bowl to accelerate the cooling process. As the wax cools it contracts and shrink cavities will appear. These cavities should be opened with a knife to allow filling with more liquid wax. Do not fill beyond the original wax level. Do not try to remove the candle from the mould until you are sure that it is fully hardened. To de-mould the candle, remove the sealant

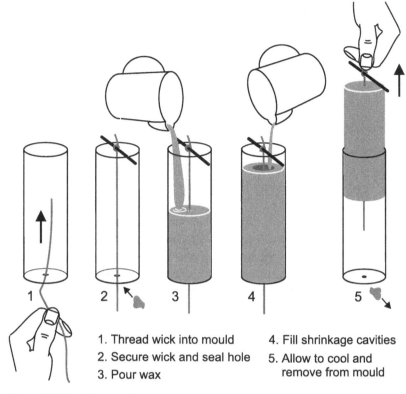

1. Thread wick into mould
2. Secure wick and seal hole
3. Pour wax
4. Fill shrinkage cavities
5. Allow to cool and remove from mould

Figure 5.7 Moulding candles

and whilst gripping the wick at the bottom of the candle, pull the candle from the mould. The candle should pull out of the mould easily, however if it is sticking it can be placed in cold water or a refrigerator to encourage some sudden shrinkage, which will help to release the candle from the mould. If there is still a problem with de-moulding, the candle can be melted out with hot water, but this will probably spoil the surface finish.

Moulding equipment: Candle moulds are readily available from candlemakers' suppliers. They are produced in two varieties, rigid and flexible. Rigid moulds are made from materials such as metal, glass and rigid plastic, whereas flexible moulds are made from stretchy materials like silicone rubbers. Flexible moulds can

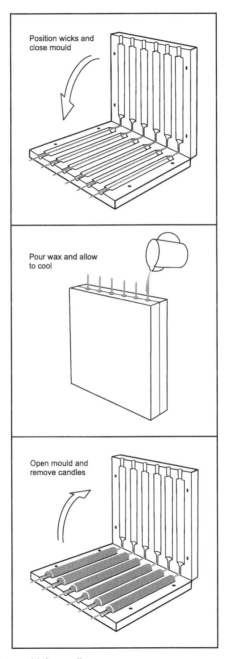

Figure 5.8 Moulding multiple candles

be used to produce irregular-shaped candles and they also allow for shapes with undercuts. Moulds are available for purchase in a wide range of shapes and sizes, but they can also be designed and made to the candlemaker's own design. Remember that the candle will be an exact replica of the internal shape and texture of the mould. If rigid moulds are used repeatedly they should be made from a material that is durable and that can be cleaned easily (glass or metal). Moulds with smooth surfaces must be treated with care as scratches and other blemishes will show on the finished candle. Multiple moulds, which make several candles at once, are a practical option where larger volume production is required.

Colours and effects: Candles can be moulded in any colour or can be poured in several different coloured layers to make horizontally striped candles. Experimenting with tilting the mould between multi-coloured layers can produce angled striped effects. Other ideas can be explored such as filling the mould with chunks of solid wax or ice cubes and then filling with liquid wax, or by experimenting with adding small amounts of solid dye before the wax has hardened. Candles with multiple wicks, or decorated with water-based transfers (decals) are also possible.

Container candles

Container candles (also known as votive candles) are extremely simple to produce and are popular as decorative items and they are usually scented. In their most basic form they are made by simply pouring wax into a heat resistant container with a central wick. They are relatively quick and simple to make because there is no dipping or de-moulding required and they are therefore often commercially successful.

Choosing appropriate containers for the production of container candles is important. The container must be safe, even when the candle has been burning for a long period. Heat resistant materials such as metal tins, ceramics and glass are ideal, although care must be taken with glass as it sometimes has a tendency to crack or shatter when heated. The selection of wax is also important, as it should be a type of wax that burns slowly and that has low

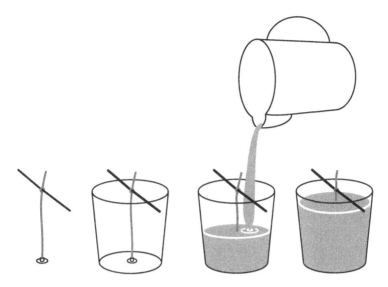

1. Attach wick sustainer to wick and position in container

2. Poor wax, allow to cool and trim wick

Figure 5.9 Container candles

shrinkage. If the wax shrinks too much as it sets in the container it will not stay in place and may come loose or form ugly sinkholes around the wick as it cools. Most natural waxes are ideal for container candles, and beeswax is excellent.

While the wax is melting, prime a wick that is slightly longer than the depth of the container and attach a small weight to the bottom of the wick (purpose made metal wick sustainers are ideal). Suspend the wick centrally in the container. If scent and colour are required add them to the liquid wax and stir. Carefully pour the liquid wax into the container to the desired level and allow the wax to cool slowly. The wick is then trimmed and the candle is complete.

Colours and scents: The appeal of container candles is usually a combination of visual beauty and aromatic fragrance. Use colours that complement the scents and try adding embedded decoration such as flowers or petals. Well-considered packaging will also enhance the marketability of your container candle designs.

Gel container candles: Gel wax container candles can be made using a similar method to other container candles, however there are some important additional considerations. The wick should be slightly thicker than you would use for paraffin wax, and must be either bought as suitable for gel wax, or primed by yourself in liquid gel wax. Wicks primed in paraffin wax will result in a cloudy candle. The gel wax itself will have to be melted at a high temperature of about 95°C so great care must be taken, and the temperature closely regulated. If embedded decoration is required this should be positioned in the bottom of the container away from the wick before the wax is poured. Normal candle dye can be used to tint the clear wax, but very small quantities are needed. Also be aware that air bubbles can be a particular problem with gel wax, especially the higher density types. To avoid bubbles take the following precautions, prime the wick properly in hot gel wax, pre-dip decorative embedment, stir and pour the wax slowly and steadily and allow to cool slowly. When using scents with gel wax, note that gel candles burn at a high temperature and this has a significant effect on the scents that can be used. For safety reasons it is therefore highly advisable to buy scents that are specifically designed for use in gel wax.

Summary

The materials and techniques described in this chapter are by no means exhaustive. They can be adapted and experimented with depending upon your own knowledge, experience and the equipment you have at your disposal. However, when developing your production processes be careful to get the right balance between the quality and beauty of your product, as compared to the speed and reliability of the making process. Most candlemakers are able to design and make a desirable product, but it is much more challenging to make larger production numbers, quickly and with consistent quality.

CHAPTER 6

Premises, workspace and stock control

One of the early tasks when starting a candlemaking enterprise is identifying and setting up a suitable premises. This chapter explains what should be considered when choosing a suitable workspace, how it should be set-up, and what to think about regarding your stock control systems.

Premises

Most new entrepreneurs will be keen to keep their overheads (fixed costs) as low as possible so will not want to incur a high monthly rental bill for their business premises. With this in mind, you may wish to get started in a building that you already own or have free access to. If you are not fortunate enough to have such a space, you will need to look into renting or buying suitable dedicated premises. The premises you choose will not only have to fit your own business needs, but you will also need to be sure that the property owner is prepared to allow your candlemaking activities to take place in their building. You may need to reassure them that the planned production processes are safe and describe any precautions you are taking to avoid risks to their property.

Costing a premises

When considering your premises options, rental charges will probably be uppermost in your mind. Business premises are often rented on a price per square meter, but you must also make sure you understand what, if any, services are included in the rental charges. If you are uncertain about signing a rental agreement it may be worth asking a legal adviser to look through it with you before you commit yourself. Remember that in addition to rent, governments in many countries impose taxes on business premises (also known as business rates). Make sure you include any business taxes in your costings when choosing a business premises. There are sometimes exemptions or reduced rates of tax for new or small businesses, so it may be worth enquiring about these with your local authorities.

Consider the services you require

Make sure the following services are adequate for your needs:

- *Access to electricity.* Is the building connected to electricity and does it have a separate electricity meter? Do you require a high capacity supply for machinery etc?
- *Mains gas.* Is there a gas supply and a separate gas meter? If a gas supply is not present bottled gas cylinders are usually a good alternative.
- *Water.* Is there a water charge, is the plumbing in good condition, and is the supply reliable?
- *Phone/computer line.* Is there a suitable connection for your equipment and are there installation and line rental charges?

Insurance and security

Insuring your premises may be a legal requirement depending upon your specific situation. If you plan to start off by working from home, you should check that your existing insurance covers you adequately. When enquiring about insurance relating to your premises you will need to consider issues such as insuring the building (especially against fire risk), the contents, including materials and stock, and the security of the building against break-ins. If you are renting premises ask the owner/agent if insurance cover is provided, and if so what specifically it covers. You will need to assure yourself that the workspace you are using is adequately secure, and there may be some costs involved in upgrading security features.

Workspace layout

When selecting a workspace it is important to carefully consider the activities that will take place in the building and the various space requirements within the business premises. You may want to consider partitioning parts of the workspace to achieve the individual spaces required. Remember the needs of disabled people and any associated equal access legislation.

Consider spaces for the following:

- *Production and packing space.* This will be dependent upon the type and number of candles you are making and the number of people working at any one time.
- *Storage space.* For raw materials, tools and equipment, and finished products and packaging (cool dark and dry space for stock).
- *Retail space.* If you intend to sell your candles directly from the workshop you will need a clean and presentable retail display area or dedicated showroom with good customer access.
- *Office space.* Many small businesses start off by doing the business administration activities from home, but others will want an office space with telephone and computer facilities within the main business premises.
- *Others.* Bathroom, toilet, kitchen, staff rest area.

Once you know the size and shape of your workspace you can start to design the layout with reference to the list above. A floor plan may be useful. Consider the space required for each anticipated activity and the most frequent actions that people will need to make during the production process, e.g. it makes sense to ensure that the wax heating equipment is conveniently positioned near to the wax pouring area. Also give thought to the movement of people across the workspace. Analyse the anticipated repetitive processes and try to design the space in a way that eliminates people crossing each other's paths, especially where hot wax is being used. Good ventilation is also required, especially where large quantities of wax are being heated. In some instances an extractor fan system will be necessary. Take measures to stop dirt and dust contaminating the candlemaking area, which should be as clean and dust free as possible.

As you design your workspace, you will almost certainly find that you require large areas of horizontal work surfaces that are level, sturdy and easy to clean. You will also want large areas of substantial shelving for materials and stock. Lighting is also an important consideration. Make good use of natural light from windows if you have it. Natural light is highly desirable for a pleasant working environment and to allow dyed wax colours to be easily assessed and monitored. Low energy strip lighting illuminating each work area is useful, and if possible use separate switches to avoid unnecessary electricity usage.

Safety

The risk of fire is the obvious safety concern associated with candle-making. Think carefully about how fires or burn injuries may be caused and design the workspace to minimize these risks. Have plenty of free space above the heating area and ensure the heating equipment is safe, well maintained and kept reasonably clean, so that residual spilt wax does not build up. Use containers for wax that are stable and easy to handle safely. Do not store flammable materials near the heating equipment and position a fire blanket and a fire extinguisher appropriately. Fit a smoke alarm to detect overheating wax and have a first aid kit easily available. Make sure that staff know how to respond in the case of a fire, and how to administer first aid for burns and other possible injuries. Once these standard precautions are in place undertake a risk analysis.

Also remember that injury can occur from many other workshop activities such as accessing high storage shelves or moving heavy and bulky items. Pay special attention to electrical cables and other trip hazards. Design into your layout reasonable working space and provide proper equipment and clothing for the required tasks. After setting up the workshop and using it for production, it is good practice to periodically review any safety risks that you think exist and take action to reduce them as far as possible. You may be required to offer access to health and safety officers, or similar government inspectors, and to show that you have carried out appropriate risk assessments and have the necessary warning signs and information displayed.

Stock control

Your stock is made up of all the items your business has ready to be sold and also all the raw materials and other items your business keeps for making products. Stock control is the process of organizing and recording your stock levels. It is useful to know your stock levels so as to:

- Keep stock at the appropriate levels (with regard to customer demand and your cashflow).
- Know when is the right time to re-order materials.
- Keep stock in good condition (old stock may deteriorate).
- Prevent stock from being lost or stolen.

The general objective is to keep as little stock as possible whilst having sufficient items so that you do not run out. This is a fine balance and keeping good stock records will help. You should set up a simple system to record both incoming and outgoing stock, and make sure all staff involved are keeping records up-to-date.

Incoming stock

When you make business purchases or take a delivery of materials, you are receiving stock. This incoming stock should be inspected as soon as possible to see that it contains the correct items. The items should be counted and their condition checked and then recorded. Delivery staff are often in a hurry, but take time to open packages to check before signing delivery notes. If there are any discrepancies against your order, record them on the delivery paperwork and inform the supplier quickly.

Outgoing stock

As sales are made stock will be moved out of the business. This must also be carefully recorded as part of your stock control system.

Breakages and damaged stock can also be recorded as outgoing stock (see Figure 6.1).

Storing and arranging stock

This is particularly important if you are producing a large range of candles, or variations within a range such as different sizes, colours or scents. If possible allocate a specific stock storage area that is logically organized so counting stock is easy. The stock storage area should remain cool and dry all year and be free from sunlight or artificial light which may cause fading of candle colours or packaging. Try to pack your newly made candles as soon as they are completed. Pack them in standard batches of a known quantity, preferably in quantities that can be sold to your customers without repacking (e.g. boxes of 12).

Keeping stock records

Stock records are kept in a stock book or file made up of a series of stock cards or sheets. Each card will record a separate candle product or raw material. This must be up-dated whenever that item comes in or goes out (see Figure 6.1). You should remake

STOCK CARD

Product: Taper Candle
Colour: Ruby Red
Size: 8 inch
Remake level: 12 or fewer

Date	Details	Stock In	Stock Out	Balance
03/04	Brought Forward		35	
11/04	Sold		3	32
21/04	Sold		12	20
29/04	Sold		10	10
09/05	Made	36	46	
14/05	Sold		12	34
14/05	Broken		6	28
19/05	Sold		12	16

Figure 6.1 Example stock card

or reorder when the figure in the balance column falls below the remake/reorder level which you have set yourself. When estimating reorder levels remember that your suppliers will sometimes be out of stock themselves or make late or wrong deliveries. Also be aware of annual fluctuations in sales that will impact on stock levels.

Stock-taking

Stock-taking is the process of counting, weighing or measuring all your stock at one time and recording the stock level and value. Stock-taking is most important for retailers or businesses that handle a wide selection and large number of products. A small-scale candlemaker will not need to conduct full stock-takes frequently so long as they keep their stock card records up to date and accurate. If you feel that your stock records have become inaccurate or neglected, for example, due to an unexpectedly busy period, you may decide to conduct a stock take during a quieter time.

CHAPTER 7

Innovation, design and intellectual property

In this chapter we look at how innovation and design development can be achieved as a means to increasing the competitiveness of your business, and keeping you ahead of the competition. We also consider emerging markets and the protection of intellectual property.

Being creative

There are such an array of theories and opinions about design creativity that it is beyond the scope of this book to offer an in depth analysis of the creative process. However, below are some useful ideas and practical methods, which can be applied to a small business that plans to devise new products, or to develop inventive production or marketing ideas.

Create space for innovation

The clichéd image of a light bulb going off in your head as a fantastic new idea appears out of nowhere is somewhat misleading. In reality, creative thinking seldom happens by pure accident, or in the course of your usual daily business routine. More often it is a result of a wholly conscious attempt to think outside or beyond the conventional norms. For this reason, if you want to nurture creative thought as a part of your business activities, the first step is simply to allocate time and space for creativity, away from the normal hectic work programme. You are then free to apply some methods of simulating lateral thinking and generating exciting ideas.

Simple ways to stimulate creative ideas

Sitting in a room and saying, 'I am now going to be creative' is usually one sure way of producing a totally blank mind! For this reason, it is a good idea to start with some kind of stimulating explanation of what you are trying to achieve.

The design brief

A useful way to give the creative process a structured starting point is to first write a design brief. This is not intended to confine your thinking, but it will offer direction to the process by stating in general terms the purpose of the exercise, or the problem that needs to be solved. A more broadly expressed design brief will allow for wider and more diverse ideas, where as a tight design brief will be more focused and usually elicit a more specific response. For example:

Broad design brief: To design a unique new range of candles for the luxury retail market.

Tight design brief: To reduce by 15 minutes the production time of 100 standard pillar candles.

However broad or tight the design brief, the process of inventive and creative thought can be equally well applied. A multitude of creative thinking methods and triggers can be referenced at this stage, but below are five examples that are applicable and practical to the candlemaking context:

1. *Ideas generation.* Get a group of people together to generate as many different and unusual ideas as possible. List the ideas but do not assess or judge them in any way at this stage. The purpose is to create an atmosphere with an abundance of ideas that people can feed from later. Encourage people to think laterally and not to restrict or sensor their ideas. It is often useful to use prompts such as mad or whacky questions (e.g. What would the candle look like if it was designed by a five year old child? How would the candle look if it were designed for a princess? Etc.).

2. *Involving outside people.* Try to include people in the creative thinking process that are not usually part of your day-to-day business. This should provide you with a different perspective and some new thoughts. Identify people who have lively and inventive minds but not necessarily those that have detailed prior knowledge or preconceptions about your enterprise activities. For example, you could involve people who represent your target customers.

3. *Explore materials.* Creative activity will often take place in the candle workshop itself, especially where new product ideas and development are concerned. Like a sculptor who knows his/her materials, the candlemaker can explore the properties of his/her materials and how they behave when used in different and unconventional ways. Experimentation and manipulation can often spark new ideas that can sometimes be developed into commercially viable products or decorative effects. It is also useful to pay attention to any unexpected results or mistakes in the workshop, which can sometimes be converted into ideas for product innovations.

4. *Observe and adapt.* Become a keen observer of everything to do with your candlemaking business. Some people find it useful to carry a notebook or small camera to remind them of things they see when they are out and about. Most new ideas are in fact a subconscious bringing together of thoughts and observations from a large number of previous experiences. It is of course illegal to copy other people's designs directly (to infringe intellectual property), but to take inspiration from your own observations is a normal creative activity. Often a relatively small innovation or adaptation to an existing design can prove more commercially viable than a radical new concept that the market is not yet ready for.

5. *Respond to opportunities.* Take advantage of the fact that your business is small and can therefore attend to market changes quickly and in a more responsive way than larger candle producers. Be alert to opportunities arising where you may be able to offer special or customized designs. For example, you might be able to quickly design a new product

for an up-coming event like a celebrity wedding or a special festival.

Critically assessing new ideas

For many new entrepreneurs the process of creating and developing ideas is the most exciting and rewarding part of their business activities. The danger, therefore, can sometimes be that the entrepreneur gets carried away with innovation and too much time and money is wasted on ideas that will never be a commercial success. For this reason it is very important to critically assess emerging ideas as they progress through the development process. The checklist of questions below has been designed to safeguard against partially resolved or weak designs being taken too far:

- Does the new design fulfil known customer needs and have sample customers reacted favourably?
- Has the design been properly costed and is the proposed retail price and profit margin acceptable?
- Is the design part of a range of products (sizes/colours)? If so what implications are there for production, packaging, advertising etc?
- Is the candle durable enough to reach the customer undamaged, or will it require special packaging?
- Is the design safe and have samples been test burnt? Are the candles stable, will they need special holders?
- What is the cost of materials for bulk production?
- Are any additional moulds or equipment required for production?
- What is the estimated production time for bulk production? This must include time for all aspects of the process e.g. melting the wax, preparing wicks, pouring/dipping, cooling, topping up and de-moulding, trimming, finishing and packing.
- What is the skill level required to produce the designs? Are there staff training implications?
- Will the quality be consistent and what is the likely reject rate?

- How will the candles be displayed and packaged for retail? Is the packaging designed and costed and does it include the required safety warnings?
- How will the products be packaged for bulk distribution? What is the weight for distribution and/or mailing?

Keep on innovating

When your business is new you will probably find that most customers will be prepared to at least consider your product range. However, as time passes, existing customers especially will be looking for up-dated and fresh product ideas. For this reason it is important to view product innovation as an ongoing business activity rather than something that is confined to the business start-up period. Remember that most of your competitors will be adapting and changing their products from time to time, and you will have to do the same if you are not to fall behind, and ideally you will become known for exciting new ideas! Also remember that innovations in production can increase productivity and therefore profitability. Sometimes a rethinking of, or adjustment to the making process can be of significant long-term benefit.

Designing for fair trade, organic and ethical markets

There are now a huge range of products designed to appeal to customers who wish to express their personal values and beliefs through their purchasing decisions. These consumers are often concerned about the health issues and wider environmental impact associated with a product's production, distribution and consumption. They may also be interested in the conditions and standards experienced by workers who are involved in the product manufacture. Many companies now create products that will appeal to this 'ethical' market and there are certainly opportunities for small candlemakers in this field.

Some customers are keen to support locally produced products. This may be because they are concerned about the environmental impact of emissions caused by transporting products long distances, particularly by airfreight. Additionally some customers like to support their own community and the local economy and are inclined to buy from local producers for that reason. If you have a sales outlet directly from your candlemaking workshop, many customers will be delighted to see how the products on display are actually produced. You may also wish to sell at local events and markets (e.g. local farmers' markets) where customers like to purchase from enterprises in their own community.

Fair trade

Some sectors of the worldwide consumer market are increasingly concerned about issues of fair trade. They want to avoid buying products from exploitative companies, which they feel are mistreating their workers with low pay and sub-standard employment rights and conditions. This offers responsible small businesses the opportunity to market themselves positively, as ethical organizations with good employment and environmental standards. Some candlemakers may even want to apply to be officially recognized for their high standards, through a process of certification. This process is usually carried out by an external body, but unfortunately can be prohibitively rigorous and time consuming for some small producers. Hence there are currently very few candles on the market that hold the official international fairtrade mark, although there are some examples of producers in Thailand whose products are certified. An alternative approach is for small candlemakers to use simple promotional tools such as leaflets and labels that clearly state their environmental and employment credentials in a factual and honest way. This can be enhanced with photographs of the making process and backed up with information about the materials used and their origins.

Natural wax candles

Candle consumers are becoming increasingly well informed about the variety of natural wax products now available, and candlemakers would be wise to be aware of these trends. One of the most popular natural waxes is soya wax, which is derived from the plant well known for yielding soya beans. Candles made from soya are preferred by customers who want to avoid carbon-based paraffin wax, and like the idea of a plant based alternative. Proponents of soya candles argue that they are a healthy product, which burn with less soot and less toxins than paraffin wax. They also point out that soya is biodegradable, spillages are easy to clean, and it is a renewable resource. Soya wax is nearly always made into container candles that are usually scented, sometimes with essential oils, and are often marketed as a luxurious natural product.

Scented candles

It is no coincidence that the market place is swamped with a huge choice of scented candles. This is because they are not only very popular with consumers, but they are also simple to produce. Most scented candles are produced in either glass or metal containers, which are often attractively labelled or boxed to increase the perceived value of the product. Candle suppliers now offer a huge range of concentrated liquid scents, which are easy to mix into wax while it is melting. Scents as diverse as bubblegum, coconut and caramel are available, but the most common ranges usually feature more sophisticated and soothing aromas like camomile, jasmine or sandalwood, amongst others. Often the candle is coloured and the packaging printed to complement the scent. There is always scope for candlemakers to be inventive, as there is always scope to blend scents together and to devise new themes and names for candle ranges that can compete successfully in the aromatic candle market.

Intellectual property, protecting your ideas

Any genuinely new designs, images, written work or means of production that you create are your own intellectual property and can therefore be protected against copying (or plagiarism) by national and international law. Some intellectual property protection is automatic, but others have to be applied for. The amount of time and money you spend on protecting your intellectual property is up to you. Apart from taking advantage of simple and free precautions, it is probably only worth pursuing comprehensive protection if you create something which is of significant commercial value, and that is likely to be copied by a third party at significant disadvantage to you. As a general rule it is advisable to keep all original documentation of your new ideas. Original sketches, samples and prototypes should be dated, signed and stored if they have future commercial potential. You can also deposit these with a responsible third party, such as a lawyer or a trade organization that offers a design repository service. Intellectual property protection is sometimes criticised by small entrepreneurs because it can be costly to secure and then cost even more if you have to use the legal process to uphold your rights against an infringement. That said, there are some practical and inexpensive safeguards that small businesses can use to deter copying.

Different countries

The systems of intellectual property protection will differ from country to country, but most tend to be designed around a common model and have more similarities than differences. It is advisable for new entrepreneurs to briefly familiarize themselves with the rules in their own country, and regionally and internationally if appropriate. Most governments have a department managing intellectual property issues and most have helpful information leaflets and websites.

Copyright

Copyright protection is automatic and free in most countries of the world. It protects creations such as written work and photographs from being used without the owner's permission. It protects only the piece of work created and not the ideas behind it. You cannot copyright a name, title, slogan or phrase. In most countries the copyright symbol is not a requirement, but it is recommended as a deterrent. The © symbol should be followed by the name of the creator and the year. Candlemakers should apply the © symbol to their published and promotional materials, especially to photographs and on website materials.

Design Right and Registered Design

In many countries there are specific systems of protection for the aesthetics of a design (sometimes called Industrial Design) that are useful in guarding against others copying the visual appearance of a new design. Design Right covers the way an object looks; its shape, colour, texture and visual appeal, and is therefore probably the most relevant protection in the field of candlemaking. It gives you automatic and free protection provided that the design is original and not a copy or adaptation of an existing design. Design Right allows you to stop anyone from copying the shape or config-uration of the product, but does not give you protection for any two-dimensional aspects of the design such as surface decoration, or patterns. Registered Design is similar to Design Right but offers slightly stronger protection. Unlike Design Right, if an infringement occurs no evidence of copying is needed providing the infringing product 'creates the same overall impression'. Registered Design is renewable for up to 25 years and applications require images, documentation and a small fee.

Patents

The most comprehensive intellectual property protection is afforded by the patent system, but this is only applicable to genuine innovations that have not previously been in the public domain. Patents relate to concepts rather than a product's appearance and are renewable, giving up to 20 years protection. For a successful application your idea must be new, inventive, and capable of commercial application. In practice patentable innovations in candle design are rare, although there are more examples and scope for patentable new production methods. The application process is relatively involved and most people will require legal assistance in drafting an application. Unfortunately patent application is therefore often considered to be beyond the means of many small enterprises, especially if their idea does not offer guaranteed commercial potential.

CHAPTER 8

Case studies

This chapter features three case studies on candlemaking enterprises, including my own business, The Wax Studio. The businesses are from three different countries (and three continents), Swazi Candles in Swaziland, Jyoti's Candles in Nepal and The Wax Studio in the UK. As you will see, although the enterprises are quite different in size and location, they also have a number of characteristics and challenges in common.

The Wax Studio

I started The Wax Studio in 2003 principally as a means of returning to the disciplines of craft and design that my career since art college had gradually taken me away from. After 'playing' with wax at home and making experimental and unusual candles for friends, I started to think seriously about converting my interest into a small business. I carried out some initial market research and then wrote a simple business plan. The idea behind the business was to create innovative new candle designs that were not already on the market. I was aware that trying to compete on price with standard imported candles would not be possible, but I did identify a niche for high-quality, contemporary, decorative candles, and this fitted my desire to do more hands-on design and making. I managed to rent a local garage from a friend and equipped it with basic equipment and candlemaking materials; The Wax Studio was born!

Creating the brand

The Wax Studio's brand took advantage of my background in product design and innovation. In the early years the new designs were marketed at high quality craft fairs, and by supplying a few local shops. As interest in the products grew, I was approached by people planning weddings and special events and responded with some new and exciting designs to suit this opportunity. This part of the business has developed significantly over the years, with various bespoke designs made to customer requirements.

Photo 8.1 Bespoke wedding candle
Credit: Jim Hiscox

I also designed the 'Icicle' candle range for weddings and special events. Each set of these candles provides the customer with a variety of display options and is supplied with magnetic candle holders, which are also designed and made at The Wax Studio. This design won the national UK Gift of the Year Award in 2010.

Photo 8.2 The 'Icicle' candle range

The first Christmas of trading confirmed that this time of year would represent by far the biggest annual sales opportunity for The Wax Studio. Since then, the gift market at Christmas has become a major focus for sales and production, and is an important element of each year's business planning.

Website and other marketing

The design and building of a website was a main part of the marketing plan from the outset. I decided that managing a physical shop would not be advisable because of the location of the business and the high overheads of rent and staffing as compared to the potential sales. Instead The Wax Studio invested in a website which formed the permanent point of access for customers to the business. In 2005 an online shop was added, since then online sales have been steadily growing, with a high rate of repeat custom: 'We find that people who have bought our products once will often come back to us because they appreciate the design and quality. It is quite a challenge to communicate the subtleties of the products on the website, photographs can only convey so much and some of the details of the candles textures and colours are only appreciated when the products are seen firsthand.'

I have also raised the profile of The Wax Studio by exhibiting at wedding fairs, trade fairs and selected craft fairs. The business has been featured in numerous newspaper and magazine articles, and gained valuable exposure by winning two awards in the space of two years. From online sales we now have a reasonable size database of interested customers who are willing to receive promotional information about offers and new designs.

Production techniques

The Wax Studio's production methods are intentionally unconventional. Although I base my designs on standard traditional techniques like dipping and moulding, these techniques have been adapted to create unusual and interesting results. Some of my production innovations include the making of unique candle moulds, special dipping tanks and candles with internal wire frames.

The Wax Studio's flagship range of products is the Tablet candles. These are slim rectangular candles that feature embedded wax decoration and two wicks. During production the wicks are positioned into the custom-made moulds before the liquid wax is poured. When the wax is setting, but still soft, pre-prepared decorative wax is applied to each candle. When the wax is fully set, the candles are de-moulded and the wicks are trimmed.

Photo 8.3 Pouring the wax

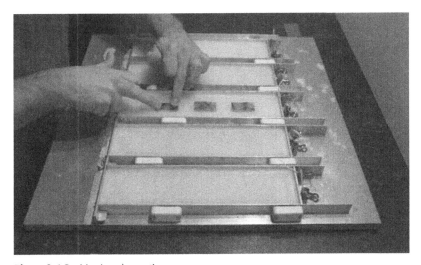

Photo 8.4 Positioning decoration

Photo 8.5 Removing candles from mould

Photo 8.6 The final product

In addition to moulded candles The Wax Studio also makes unusually long dipped candles using custom made dipping tanks. Once dipped these candles are manipulated into a variety of shapes before being allowed to set hard (such as the 'Icicle' candle range).

I also like to continue to develop new ideas and one-off designs such as my wax sculptures, which are spiral forms, hand shaped from large sheets of hand poured wax.

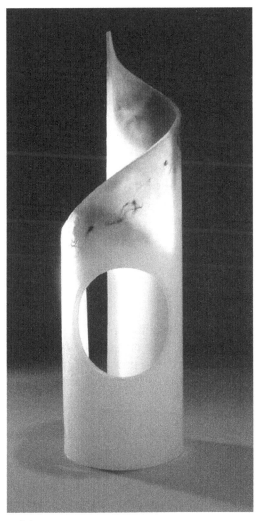

Photo 8.7 Wax sculpture

Challenges and lessons

The Wax Studio has been very successful in developing products that are highly regarded by customers for their quality and design. However making commercially viable handmade products in the UK has not been easy, mainly because of the relatively high labour and material costs. Although handmade products can attract a premium price, it has sometimes been challenging to factor in all the business costs, when estimating income from sales. When selling products direct to customers we can make a reasonable profit, but we have found selling to retail outlets has been more difficult to make viable. Although buyers are keen to stock our designs, producing and distributing candles at a price that allows for the retail mark-ups has been difficult for us to achieve, without significant expansion and higher production volumes. I first started the business to allow myself the means to design and make my own interesting products, and I have always tried to hold true to this vision. The business has always had potential to grow into something much larger, but I have consciously kept things small to avoid being drawn into becoming a business manager, rather than a designer and maker.

For more information see: www.thewaxstudio.com

Jyoti's Candles

Jyoti's Candles is a small candle manufacturer based in the city of Kathmandu in Nepal. The enterprise was started by Ms Jyoti Shrestha in 2002 in an effort to provide employment for disadvantaged girls who were looking for work in order to support the costs of their further education.

Jyoti became fascinated with candlemaking after finding herself with more free time on her hands after her children grew up and left home. She found inspiration and training from books and experts and before long began making her own candles, which, with the help of some local girls, led to the establishment of a new small business. Her ambition was to provide employment opportunities for girls to help them finance their education. In Nepal girls often

Photo 8.8 Floating candles

have to stop going to college because their families give priority
to the education of their male children. Girls often end up having
to get married or find work as housemaids. By providing work for
these girls, Jyoti is able to help them to continue their education
and open up greater opportunities for them in later life.

The business opportunity

In Nepal there is a specific demand for decorative candles, in
particular amongst the more wealthy middle classes and during the
Christmas and New Year period. Hotels and restaurants have also
started using decorative candles and they have become a popular
gift amongst the younger generations. Meditation centres also
encourage people to buy aromatic candles with natural and herbal
essence to create a relaxing atmosphere. This recent expanding
market has been largely supplied by candles imported into Nepal,
and Jyoti therefore identified an opportunity to supply the market
with locally produced, high quality products which could compete
with the imports. Jyoti started her business from home, working
with two girls, but quickly saw her business grow. She was soon
able to employ three more girls, who were looking for work to help
them pay for their college fees. The candles were initially sold at

Photo 8.9 Square moulded candles

small markets such as the Christmas Bazaar, Diwali Mela and the Woman's Handicraft Trade Fair. The products grew in popularity and before long orders were being placed by hotels, restaurants, and by companies who wanted to distribute promotional gifts during Diwali and Christmas. With the help of various Rotary Clubs and other charity organizations Jyoti's Candles also started exporting the decorative candles to Europe, providing an additional income for the sponsorship of disadvantaged students.

Marketing and product range

To begin with the marketing of the enterprise was based largely on Jyoti's personal contacts and word of mouth. Later the business progressed to producing brochures, which were circulated and emailed to places like embassies and international non-government organizations at Christmas and for Diwali. Jyoti's Candles began to receive large corporate orders during Diwali and Christmas mainly to provide candles as gifts for the clients of the corporations. Regular

Photo 8.10 Christmas candles

orders were also secured from luxury hotels and restaurants. The enterprise participated in a few exhibitions that also resulted in orders from new contacts. Most recently Jyoti's Candles has also been undertaking promotion on the internet through e-shopping websites and Facebook.

The business now summarizes its markets and products as follows:

- *Diwali candles.* Floating candles and candles for small lamps (Diya).
- *Christmas candles.* Decorative candles; thick, bright and colourful.
- *Hotels and restaurants.* Slim with detailed finishing for dining tables.
- *Exhibitions and charity.* Various decorative candles.
- *Utility candles.* For households during electrical power cuts.

Production techniques and materials

When girls join Jyoti's Candles for employment they generally have no craft-making experience. The business therefore uses simple candle moulding production techniques, which can be taught quickly whilst ensuring good quality and consistent product results can be achieved. The uncoloured paraffin wax is melted in double boilers on domestic gas stoves to around 90°C and the required colour and scent is added. The wicks are positioned in the moulds and then the wax is poured. Once the wax is set hard the candles are removed from the moulds and finished. Jyoti says, 'In general, the candles are not manufactured in a regular production line; instead we make on a demand basis, as per client orders. That way we know we will sell what we have made and we do not have to worry about storing large quantities of stock'. One of the constraints for the production side of the business is the restricted supply of materials and equipment. Presently the capacity for creating moulds and designs for decorative candles in Nepal is limited. Good quality moulds are not manufactured in Nepal and locally made ones lack the quality and finish of imported moulds from India or Europe. The raw materials (wax and wicks) are also not available locally and have to be imported from China. This reliance on imported goods increases the cost of the candles, making it difficult to compete with the price of imported products. A particular concern is the quality of wicks. Jyoti says 'We have occasionally had complaints about wicks from international clients who insist on high quality products'.

Challenges and lessons

Jyoti's Candles is constantly working to maintain a competitive advantage for their products because increasing numbers of decorative candles are being imported into Nepal. This is in an environment where the market size for decorative candles is fairly narrow, and it is always a challenge to find a stable demand. For this reason it is financially risky to invest heavily in the business and Jyoti therefore finds it difficult to commit to employing staff on a long-term basis. She explains, 'To ensure the sustainability of the business it is important to be creative and active. To compete with tough competition we need to standout with good quality and creative products. The company must remain up-to-date with the latest techniques and designs. This requires things like web-research, market demand studies and interaction with key clients such as the ex-pat community'. Furthermore, Jyoti says, 'For corporate business, extra care must be taken with quality as well as the timely delivery of products to ensure that orders are received without delay. Communication between staff members also has to be effective and they need to be well trained in the manufacturing process, reducing damage to candles and minimizing material waste'.

Swazi Candles

Photo 8.11 The Swazi Candles shop sign

Swazi Candles was started in an old cowshed of a former dairy, in 1981 by two South African art graduates, Tony Marshak and Bernard Abramowitz. In those days the Kingdom of Swaziland, which is completely landlocked by South Africa and Mozambique, was a haven of freedom and refuge from the apartheid regime in South Africa, and along with its remarkable mountainous countryside, proved an attractive setting for Tony and Bernard to start their business. From these humble beginnings Swazi Candles has gradually grown into an important attraction for visitors to Swaziland and is also now a well-known international brand of handmade decorative candles.

Products

With their background in art and design, Tony and Bernard have always been interested in creating new products, and they have successfully developed a very distinctive style for which their candle range is now well known. Their production technique

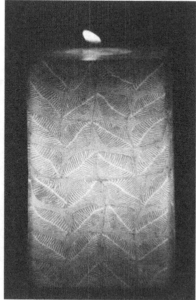

Photo 8.12 and **8.13** Swazi decorative candles

uses a process known as 'millefiore' or 'thousand flowers' which is an ancient decorative technique, revived in the 18th century by the glassmakers of Italy and later made famous in the African glass bead trade. Swazi Candles has cleverly adapted the art of millefiore, replacing glass with a hard wax to make their characteristic colourful surface designs. The decorative wax is applied in sheets to the outer surface of the candles and then when the candle is lit, the flame glows through the hard outer surface creating a radiant lantern effect.

Swazi Candles also produce an amazingly wide range of African animal-shaped candles, the surfaces of which are also covered with a variety of millefiore decoration. Visitors to the Swazi Candle shop can watch the skilled artisans shaping these candles from warm wax, and this allows customers to buy the very candle they have watched being made. Tony points out that the vast range of shapes and sizes is both a strength and weakness, 'Customers love to see the amazing array of designs, but it makes putting together a product catalogue almost impossible!'

Photo 8.14 Animal candles awaiting packaging

Handmade production and employment

Swazi Candles are proud of their tradition of handmade production. When they first moved from South Africa to establish the business they found the Swazi people open and receptive to training, and able to develop into fine handicraft workers and skilled artisans. The labour intensive nature of the production meant that Tony and Bernard were able to provide much needed employment in Swaziland, and at its peak in the mid-nineties they provided jobs for over 200 local people. In addition to just jobs, Swazi candles has always been very concerned about the working conditions and wider social welfare of their employees. Tony says, 'Our workers are part of the decision-making processes and we have systems of health care, pension funds, funeral insurance, and food and travel allowances in place'. Although offering these benefits is a significant cost to the business, Swazi Candles believe strongly in the principals of fair trade and they are members of WFTO (World Fair Trade Organization), which is also an increasingly valuable marketing attribute.

Photo 8.15 Swazi Candles employees packaging candles

Markets

Over the years Swazi Candles has been successful in building a distinct brand that is now established in many parts of the world. From their humble beginning selling to local hotels and shops, they started their own retail shop in 1982. The shop proved very popular with visitors to Swaziland and still remains a very important source of income for the business today, providing about 30 per cent of sales. The shop also plays an important role in Swaziland's tourist industry more generally. Swazi Candles were aware that the local market was limited in size and they were keen to expand into new export markets. In 1998 they gradually started showing their products at trade fairs in Europe and America, where the distinctly Swazi ethnic style of the products found new markets. The product quality and consistency was improved to meet market demands and by the year 2000 they were shipping six to eight containers a year to distributors and shops in America and Europe.

Challenges and lessons

Swazi Candles had a period of rapid growth in the late nineties and early 2000's. They recruited 50 per cent more employees and bigger premises were acquired to cope with the increased production. This expansion was successful for a period of about five years, but the pace of growth, although encouraging, also created new challenges. Tony recalls how in 2004 one of Swazi Candles biggest customers in the USA stopped sending them orders, almost overnight. This left the business with under utilized capacity and disproportionally high overheads. Unfortunately the difficult decision to make unavoidable redundancies had to be made. Tony and Bernard still recall that period as a very difficult time, not only for the business, but for themselves personally. They are now slightly more wary of rapid expansion.

For more information see: www.swazicandles.com

Further information sources

Candlemaking books

There are a huge number of candlemaking books produced for the hobby market. They usually include information about materials, equipment and step-by-step instructions for a variety of simple candlemaking techniques, often illustrated with colour photographs. Some books deal with one specific method only, such as dipping, or one specific material, such as beeswax. Most books are designed for use by people making candles at home, and some include information about making candle holders and decorative candle displays.

Constable, D (1997) *Beginners Guide to Candlemaking,* Search Press, Kent.
This book features simple equipment, materials and techniques.

Constable, D (1992) *Candlemaking, Creative Designs and Techniques,* Search Press, Kent.
This book features some slightly more advanced techniques than the 'Beginners Guide'.

Oppenheimer, B (1997) *The Candlemaker's Companion: A Comprehensive Guide to Rolling, Pouring, Dipping, and Decorating Your Own Candles.*
This is a larger volume, slightly more comprehensive.

Internet resources

It is unusual to find fully independent information resources on the internet. Most information sites are sponsored by advertisers.

However some offer useful information, articles and forums. Some are also suppliers of materials and equipment.

Information and advice websites

http://www.candlecauldron.com/
A large selection of information and issues concerning candle-making (USA).

http://www.letsmakecandles.com/index.asp/
A good range of information on candlemaking with some links to suppliers, projects and ideas on selling candles (USA).

http://www.candlemakingsupplies.co.uk/
'How to' candlemaking projects with photos and links to suppliers (UK).

http://www.candlemakers.co.uk/
Includes books, videos, classes, safety information etc (UK).

http://www.candletech.com/
Basic instructions for candlemaking and soap making techniques (promoting Peak Candles Company USA).

Supplier websites

UK

http://www.4candles.co.uk/
Good range of supplies

http://www.fullmoons-cauldron.co.uk/
Large range of supplies

http://www.britishwax.com/
Industrial wax supplier

http://www.thorne.co.uk/
Beeswax

USA

http://www.peakcandle.com/
  Equipment and materials

http://www.soywaxcandles.org/
  Soya information and supplier links

http://www.soywaxcandleinfo.org/
  Soya information

South Africa

http://www.funwithcandles.co.za/index.html/
  Selection of moulds and accessories

http://www.candles.co.za/
  Candles and candlemaking supplies

http://www.simkul.co.za/
  Industrial wax supplier

India

http://www.srswax.com/about-us.html/
  Industrial waxes supplier

Organizations

http://www.britishcandlemakers.org/
  The British Candle Makers' Federation

http://www.igca.net/
  International Guild of Candle Artisans (focuses on USA)

http://www.candles.org/
  National Candle Association, USA

(All websites were accessed September 2014)

Lightning Source UK Ltd.
Milton Keynes UK
UKOW06f2319300315

248788UK00001B/3/P